WordPerfect 6
for Windows
Quick&Easy

A Visual Approach for the Beginner

Welcome to **Quick & Easy**. Designed for the true novice, this new series covers basic tasks in a simple, learn-by-doing fashion. If that sounds like old news to you, take a closer look.

Quick & Easy books are a bit like picture books. They're for people who would rather see and do than read and ponder. The books are colorful. They're full of illustrations, and accompanying text that is straightforward, concise, and easy to read.

But don't waste your time reading about our **Quick & Easy** books; start learning your new software package instead. This **Quick & Easy** book is just the place to start.

WordPerfect® 6 for Windows™

Quick & Easy

Christian Crumlish

SYBEX®

San Francisco • Paris • Düsseldorf • Soest

Acquisitions Editor: Dianne King
Developmental Editor: Steve Lipson
Editor: Brenda Kienan
Assistant Editors: Valerie Potter, Kristen Vanberg-Wolf
Technical Editor: Jim Gershfield
Book Designer: Helen Bruno
Screen Graphics Artist: John Corrigan
Page Layout and Typesetter: Ann Dunn
Production Editor: Carolina Montilla
Production Assistants/Proofreaders: Kristin Amlie, Sarah Lemas
Indexer: Ted Laux
Cover Designer: Archer Design
Cover Illustrator: Richard Miller

Screen reproductions produced with Collage Plus
Collage Plus is a trademark of Inner Media Inc.

SYBEX is a registered trademark of SYBEX Inc.

TRADEMARKS: SYBEX has attempted throughout this book to distinguish
proprietary trademarks from descriptive terms by following the capitalization
style used by the manufacturer.

SYBEX is not affiliated with any manufacturer.

Every effort has been made to supply complete and accurate information.
However, SYBEX assumes no responsibility for its use, nor for any infringe-
ment of the intellectual property rights of third parties which would result
from such use.

Library of Congress Card Number: 93-86304
ISBN: 0-7821-1406-7

Manufactured in the United States of America
10 9 8 7 6 5 4 3 2 1

To Ted Nadeau, Richard Fleming, and Sina Khajeh-Najafi

ACKNOWLEDGMENTS

●

I'd like to thank Steve Lipson, my developmental editor and successor. Thanks also to Richard Mills, who edited my first Quick & Easy book and who deserves a lot of credit for its success; and to Helen Bruno, the series designer.

I'd like to thank my editor, Brenda Kienan.

My thanks to technical editor Jim Gershfield, typesetter Ann Dunn, artist Helen Bruno, production editor Carolina Montilla, proofreaders and production assistants Kristin Amlie and Sarah Lemas, and indexer Ted Laux.

Thanks to my family and friends, who've been incredibly supportive. Thanks especially to Richard A. Frankel, my hardware guru, for helping me find the right equipment for my needs at the best possible prices.

Contents
at a Glance
●

Contents

INTRODUCTION

●

Just because you work with a computer doesn't mean you like it. Most people find computers intimidating. Sure, they're supposed to make life easier. Then again, they were also supposed to make paper obsolete. (Right.) Sometimes, a computer is just a nuisance—something else you've got to learn how to use. But it doesn't have to be that way.

Computers *are* getting easier to use, believe it or not. With Windows on your PC, you can get things done without having to know strange codes and commands or even what's really going on inside the machine. WordPerfect for Windows is a very powerful, flexible word-processing program, but in some ways it's *too* powerful. There are so many options, so many doodads on the screen, so many choices, it can be bewildering. It's not your fault if you feel confused. I'm sure it's great that someone can now put a picture inside a list inside a footnote, but are *you* ever going to do that?

This book will get you started with WordPerfect right away. I'll tell you just the things you'll need to know and steer you away from the stuff that would bog you down. You'll see how easy using a computer can be. The lessons in this book are bite-sized and easy to follow. They show you exactly what you should expect to see on the screen and tell you exactly what to do. You don't have to know anything about computers, DOS, Windows, word processing, or WordPerfect (you don't even have to know what all those things are).

What Makes It Quick and Easy?

As you can see, this book is short, under two hundred pages. The lessons are rarely longer than ten pages each. Best of all, I've eliminated all the junk you don't need to know, and believe me, you could fill a thousand-page book with the things you'll *never* use in WordPerfect. I'll always tell you the best and easiest ways to accomplish essential tasks. You'll be through this book in no time, and, in fact, after the first few lessons you'll know most of the important things about how to create documents in WordPerfect.

If you flip through this book, you'll see that there are tons of illustrations. I want you to feel confident at all times that you're on the right track and things are working the way they're supposed to. Anytime I describe something you should see on the screen, or tell you to do something, I'll show you what it should look like. You can learn almost everything just looking at the pictures! You'll also notice labels explaining items on the screen and occasional notes with helpful hints or explanations. Mainly, though, you'll learn by doing, following my step-by-step instructions.

At the beginning of each lesson is a suggested time to give you an idea of how long that lesson will take. It may go faster for you or you may want to take more time. That's okay. Nobody's holding a stopwatch.

I Won't Steer You Wrong

This book will work best for you if you follow the instructions exactly and do the lessons in order. Although it is possible to learn from the lessons without following them exactly, you'll lose some of the reassurance you get from seeing exactly the same thing on your screen as you see in the illustration on the page.

There are variations from one computer to the next, from one screen to the next, from one printer to the next. Also, if you're not the first person to use your copy of WordPerfect, the previous users may have altered the setup in ways that may make your results differ slightly from the illustrations. If the differences are minor, you might as well just ignore them. If things look seriously different, you should have someone look at your setup and possibly return it to its beginning state.

Once you start a lesson, you'll be best off if you don't make idle changes. If you do, it may be hard to get things back the way they were. If you do something wrong by mistake, you can often get out of the situation by pressing Esc (the upper-leftmost key on most keyboards).

Help on the Way

If you are ever really stuck or if you wind up with strange problems not discussed in this book, keep in mind that WordPerfect has a very good Help feature. Use the Help Index command on the Help menu when you need information. You can then click a button labeled **Instructions** to get an explanation of how to use Help.

Using Your Mouse with Windows

This book assumes you are using a mouse. If you don't have one, you can still follow most of the instructions, but I highly recommend you get one. Windows was designed to be used with a mouse. Here are a couple of mouse techniques you need to understand:

To *click* something, position the mouse pointer over that thing and then quickly press and release the left mouse button. For example, if I tell you to click the leftmost button on the Power Bar, what you do will look like this:

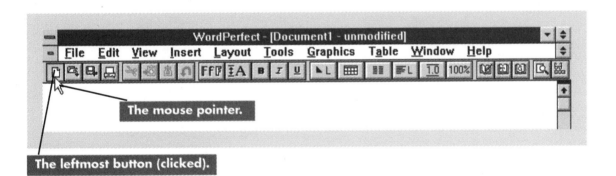

The mouse pointer.

The leftmost button (clicked).

To *double-click* something, position the mouse pointer over that thing and then quickly press and release the left mouse button twice in a row. (You can probably figure out triple-click and quadruple-click yourself. So far WordPerfect has no use for a quintuple-click, thank goodness.)

To *drag* something, position the mouse pointer over it, press the left mouse button, and then *before releasing the mouse button* move the mouse so that the thing you clicked is visibly dragged across the screen.

To *pull down* a menu and select an option on it, position the mouse pointer over a menu name in the menu bar, press the left mouse button, and then drag the mouse toward you. When the specified option on the menu is highlighted, release the mouse button. For example, if I tell you to pull down the File menu and select New, what you do will look like this:

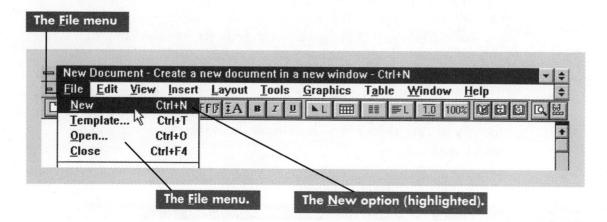

The File menu

The File menu.

The New option (highlighted).

That's all you need to know to begin. So what are you waiting for?

PART ONE

What Do I Do First?

If you are new to word processors, or to WordPerfect for Windows specifically, it may seem like there are limitless commands, terms, techniques, clicks, and what have you, that you're going to have to learn before you can really *do* anything. Not so! Almost everything you will ever do with WordPerfect comes down to a few very straightforward steps. In this part we will go through the absolute basics of word processing with WordPerfect for Windows. You will learn to start the program, type something, save what you have written, print it out, and quit. What could be simpler?

5 MINUTES

Start WordPerfect

To use a program, you have to start it first. Starting WordPerfect is easy. After you've done it once, you probably won't think about it again. I'll start from the first thing you might see on the screen, and tell you what to do from there.

Here We Go...

First of all, look at your screen. If it is blank, make sure your computer is on. If the screen is blank and the computer is on, you may have to turn the monitor on also. Look for a button below the picture tube, along the sides of the monitor, or in the back.

If Windows is already running, you can skip step 1 below. On the screen you should see something called the DOS prompt.

C:\>

This is a typical prompt. Yours may be C:> or D:\> or another variation. Prompts almost always end with >. It doesn't really matter much, because you're about to start Windows, and the whole point of Windows is that you don't have to think about things like prompts and memorized commands.

1. Type **WIN** and press ↵. Windows should start. Sit tight; it may take a minute.

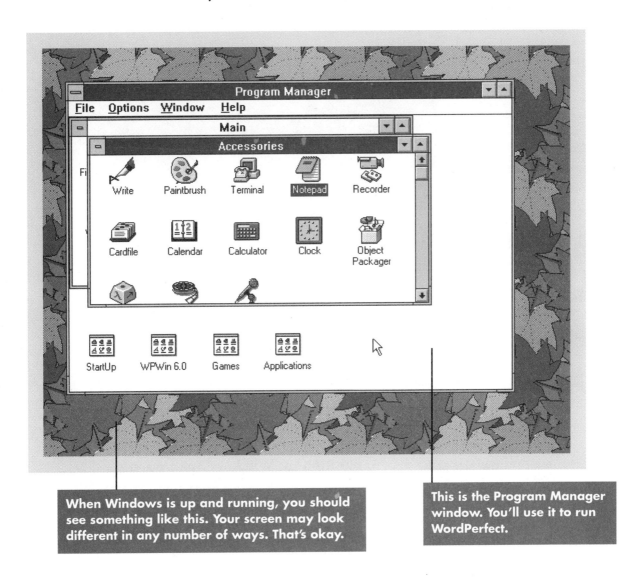

When Windows is up and running, you should see something like this. Your screen may look different in any number of ways. That's okay.

This is the **Program Manager** window. You'll use it to run WordPerfect.

If you don't see the Program Manager window open on your screen, look for the Program Manager icon at the bottom of the screen.

Here it is.

If you see the Program Manager icon, double-click on it to open the Program Manager window.

● Note Windows usually stays the way it was when you used it last. If you or anyone else ran your copy of Windows before and changed the positions of various windows or icons, then they'll still be in those new positions. So don't get excited if your screen doesn't match mine exactly.

2. Now pull down the <u>W</u>indow menu, and see if there is a menu option that reads **WPWin 6.0**. If so, select it, as shown. If not, select **Applications** or **Windows Applications**.

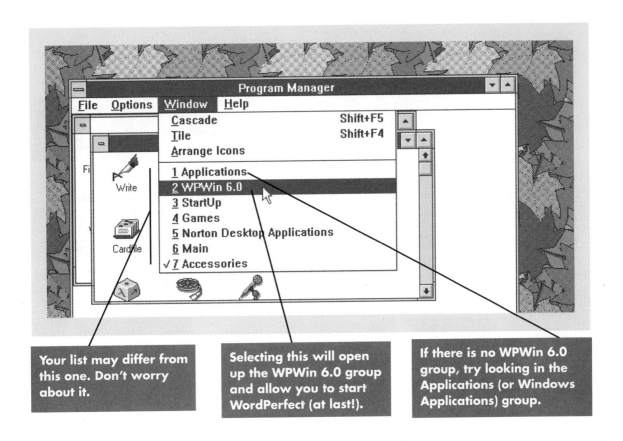

Your list may differ from this one. Don't worry about it.

Selecting this will open up the WPWin 6.0 group and allow you to start WordPerfect (at last!).

If there is no WPWin 6.0 group, try looking in the Applications (or Windows Applications) group.

In this window, you should see a WPWin 6.0 icon.

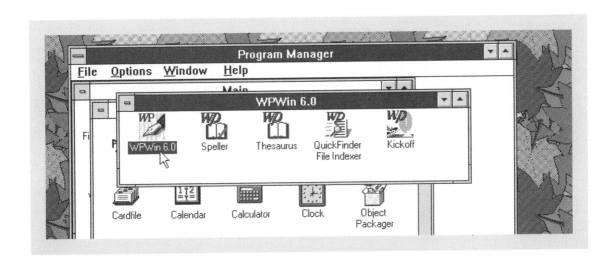

3. Double-click on the WPWin 6.0 icon and WordPerfect for
Windows will start.

First you'll see a logo with a fountain pen in the middle of the screen. Then you'll see this screen. This is
the moment we've been waiting for.

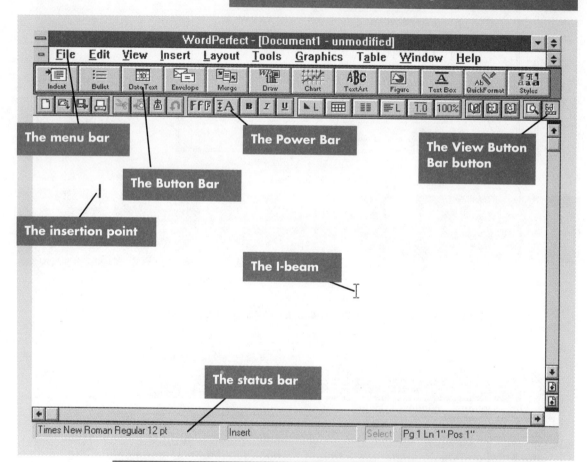

As you can see, almost everything on the WordPerfect screen has a
name. It can all seem a lot more complicated than it really is. You
could read a long, boring discussion of each of these parts of the
screen, but instead, in the next lesson, you'll jump right in and start
typing, and I'll explain anything you need to know as you go along.

You won't need to use the Button Bar for a while, but you can use all the room on the screen you can get:

4. Click the View Button Bar button (the rightmost one on the Power Bar), as shown:

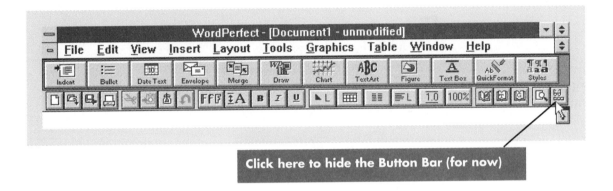

Click here to hide the Button Bar (for now)

The Button Bar disappears.

That's it for preliminaries. Now you can actually do something. In the next lesson, you'll start right in with some typing.

A Glorified Typewriter

2

For all its fancy bells and whistles, WordPerfect mainly allows you to use your computer (plus printer) as a typewriter. A very flexible typewriter, perhaps, but a typewriter nonetheless. So now it's time to do some typing.

Typing

Let's start with a simple, short example—a memo.

1. Begin by typing the first lines of a normal memo. Use your own name or make one up if you like. (Hit ↵ at the end of each line.)

MEMORANDUM ↵
To: [Tab] All Staff ↵
From: [Tab] Christian Crumlish ↵
Date: [Tab] February 27, 1994 ↵
Re: [Tab] Four-day work week ↵

● Note Don't worry about making mistakes. We're just doing typing for now. You'll learn all about how to make corrections and changes, but first things first.

2. Now, to skip a line, hit ↵ again.

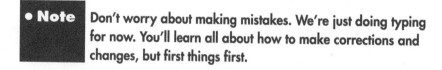

3. Type the following paragraph, but don't press ↵ when you get near the end of a line. Just keep typing. You'll see why.

> As you all know, we have been experimenting for the past month with a four-day work week. I am pleased to announce that the preliminary results are in, and so far the experiment has been an amazing success. Productivity is off the scale!

Your screen should now look something like this:

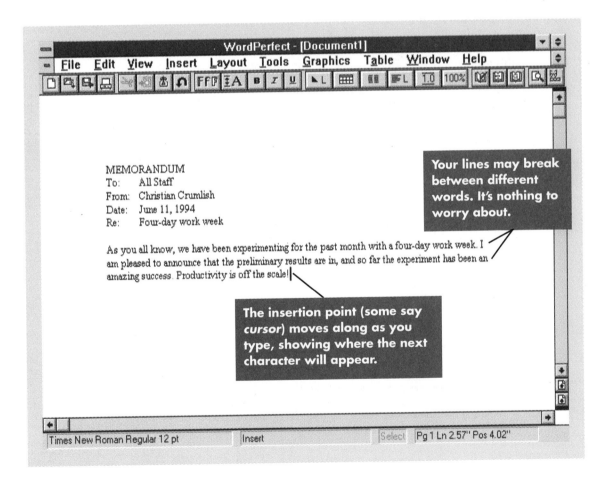

> **● Note** You have just seen one of the advantages WordPerfect offers over a typewriter, something called "word wrap." You don't need to decide when a line is full, and you don't have to worry about going "off the paper." Just type away and watch the words "wrap" from one line to the next. Use ↵ only to end paragraphs or to leave blank lines.

4. Press ↵ twice to start a new paragraph.

5. Type the following:

I'm sure I'm not the only one here who used to dread Monday morning, but I think you'll all agree that it looks a lot brighter after a three-day weekend. Because of the success of our trial run, we are going to extend the four-day work week schedule for a further six months. If all goes well, and I don't see any reason why it shouldn't, we'll make the plan permanent. ⌨↵

Your screen should look like this:

```
MEMORANDUM
To:     All Staff
From:   Christian Crumlish
Date:   June 11, 1994                          I
Re:     Four-day work week


As you all know, we have been experimenting for the past month with a four-day work week. I
am pleased to announce that the preliminary results are in, and so far the experiment has been an
amazing success. Productivity is off the scale!

I'm sure I'm not the only one here who used to dread Monday morning, but I think you'll all agree
that it looks a lot brighter after a three-day weekend. Because of the success of our trial run, we
are going to extend the four-day work week schedule for a further six months. If all goes well,
and I don't see any reason why it shouldn't, we'll make the plan permanent.
I
```

There, now you've made something called a *document*. WordPerfect considers anything you write to be a document, but putting words down on the page or the screen is often just the first step. A first draft on a computer screen has a way of looking finished just because the letters are set in type and the lines are all even, but often you'll need to revise a draft, possibly more than once. WordPerfect provides a variety of editing tools and techniques—the easiest to use, and the ones you'll take advantage of most often, are the Backspace and Delete keys.

When to Use Backspace and When to Use Delete

You'll use Backspace most of the time to make corrections on the fly. I'll take you through the process once, step by step, but you'll see that it quickly becomes second nature, and, if you're a sloppy typist, like me, it becomes part of the typing process itself.

1. Press ↵ to skip a line.

2. Type **Next experiment is telecommuting** and stop there.

3. Press Backspace thirteen times. Watch as the insertion point moves backward, eating up the word *telecommuting* one letter at a time.

I'm sure I'm not the only one here who used to dread Monday morning, but I think you'll all agree that it looks a lot brighter after a three-day weekend. Because of the success of our trial run, we are going to extend the four-day work week schedule for a further six months. If all goes well, and I don't see any reason why it shouldn't, we'll make the plan permanent.

Next experiment is |

The word *telecommuting* is gone.

4. In place of the erased word, type **working at home.** (including the period).

5. Hit ↵.

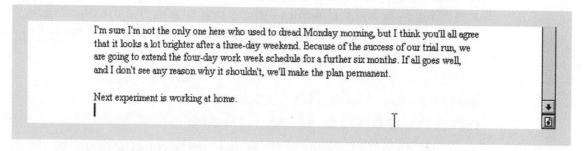

So you see, pressing Backspace erases the character to the *left* of the insertion point. This doesn't necessarily mean the letter you just typed.

6. Using the mouse, move the I-beam so it is positioned exactly between the *N* and *e* in *Next*.

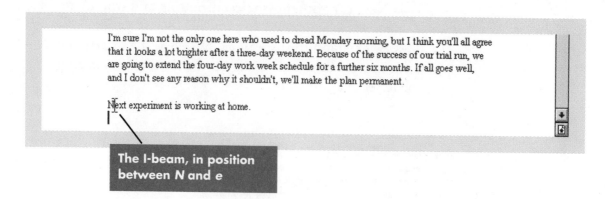

The I-beam, in position between *N* and *e*

7. Click the mouse. The insertion point appears where you clicked.

I'm sure I'm not the only one here who used to dread Monday morning, but I think you'll all agree that it looks a lot brighter after a three-day weekend. Because of the success of our trial run, we are going to extend the four-day work week schedule for a further six months. If all goes well, and I don't see any reason why it shouldn't, we'll make the plan permanent.

Next experiment is working at home.

The insertion point in its new location

8. Press Backspace once.

9. Type The n. (Don't type the period, it's one of mine.)

I'm sure I'm not the only one here who used to dread Monday morning, but I think you'll all agree that it looks a lot brighter after a three-day weekend. Because of the success of our trial run, we are going to extend the four-day work week schedule for a further six months. If all goes well, and I don't see any reason why it shouldn't, we'll make the plan permanent.

The next experiment is working at home.

The difference between Backspace and Delete is that the Delete key erases the character to the *right* of the insertion point.

10. Put the insertion point just before the *w* in *working*.

11. Hit Delete repeatedly until the rest of the line disappears.

> I'm sure I'm not the only one here who used to dread Monday morning, but I think you'll all agree that it looks a lot brighter after a three-day weekend. Because of the success of our trial run, we are going to extend the four-day work week schedule for a further six months. If all goes well, and I don't see any reason why it shouldn't, we'll make the plan permanent.
>
> The next experiment is |

> **• Note** You can also just hold down **Delete** and it will Delete many characters very quickly. This can sometimes be risky because you may erase something you didn't mean to. In this case, however, you're already at the end of the memo, so the worst thing that might happen is you might hear some warning beeps that tell you you've reached the end and there's nothing more to Delete. By the way, **Backspace** and many other keys also repeat this way when you hold them down. You might as well throw that old Selectric away.

12. Type telecommuting. (including the period) and then press ↵. (Well, I had to change it to something.)

> I'm sure I'm not the only one here who used to dread Monday morning, but I think you'll all agree that it looks a lot brighter after a three-day weekend. Because of the success of our trial run, we are going to extend the four-day work week schedule for a further six months. If all goes well, and I don't see any reason why it shouldn't, we'll make the plan permanent.
>
> The next experiment is telecommuting.
> |

So, to erase a word with Backspace, put the insertion point at the end of the word. To erase a word with Delete, put the insertion point at the beginning.

● Note If you plan to take a break before continuing, first take the time to save your memo, as explained in Lesson 3. Then, when you feel like doing some more, check Lesson 7 for how to reopen the memo and continue where you left off.

Save or You'll Be Sorry

3

One good reason to use a computer for writing is that the computer has a memory. It can store your work and you can return to it later. But the computer does not automatically remember what you do, and just because you see something on the screen is no guarantee it will be there later when you come back to it.

That's why you have to *save* your work. It's very easy to do. I'll show you that, and then I'll also show you how to save something to a floppy disk, so you can take your work from one computer to another.

Finally, I'll show you a good way to have WordPerfect save automatically, so that in case of an accident or emergency, you won't lose all the work you've done since the last time you saved.

But first, regular everyday saving.

Save Your Document for the First Time

Here's how to save the memo you typed in Lesson 2:

1. Pull down the File menu and select Save, as shown:

SAVE YOUR DOCUMENT FOR THE FIRST TIME

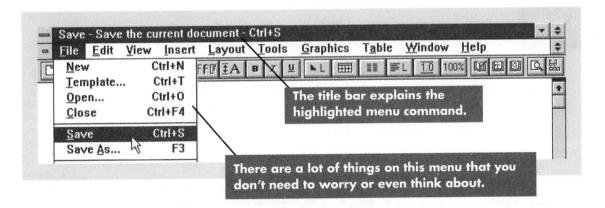

You'll see the following dialog box appear:

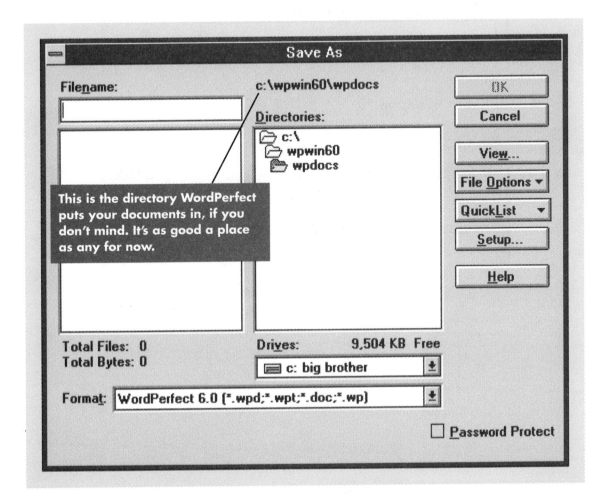

● **Note** As usual, there are all sorts of buttons and things in this dialog box that may make you queasy. Just ignore them, at least for now.

2. You have to give your document a name. Type memo (under File<u>n</u>ame:) in the dialog box:

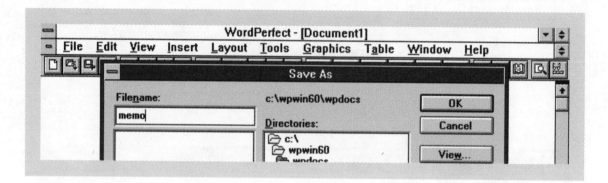

3. Click the OK button.

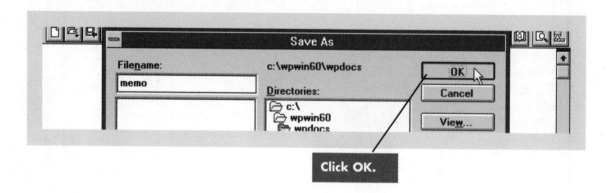

Click OK.

> **● Note** You could also press ↵. With any dialog box, if you hit the Enter key, it's just the same as if you clicked whichever button is highlighted. In this case it's the OK button. This also means that you must be careful *not* to press ↵ before you are finished entering information in a dialog box.

There, you've saved your memo. The name you give it is now in the title bar:

Notice that Wordperfect has given your memo the extension .wpd, which identifies it as a WordPerfect for Windows document.

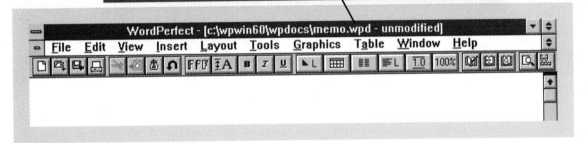

Save Changes to Your Document

If you make changes to your document, you'll need to save it again. Otherwise, the changes will be lost forever. To demonstrate this, make a minor change to the memo and then save it again.

1. Make sure the insertion point is at the end of the memo by hitting Ctrl+End.

2. Press ↵ to add another blank line to the memo. This doesn't really change the way the memo looks, but it is a real change.

3. Pull down the File menu and select Save.

WordPerfect saves your document again, in a flash. If you blink, you'll miss it. Now back to work.

Saving a Copy of Your Document

There are several reasons why you might want to make a copy of your document. If you plan to make a similar document, you can save a copy of the first and then change the copy while keeping the original unchanged. Or, if you need to work on your document on another machine, perhaps to print it out, you'll have to save a copy of the document to a floppy disk, and then carry the disk to the other computer.

If you don't have your own computer to work on, you'll usually need to save your work to a disk so that you can keep it. It's also good to keep copies of your work on disks in case there are ever problems with your computer or its *hard disk*, which is where your work is stored. Now I'll show you how to save a copy of your memo to a disk.

1. Get a floppy disk and insert it in the disk drive. (If you have more than one, insert it in the upper drive or the leftmost one.) If there is a latch or door on the drive, close it.

2. Pull down the File menu and select Save As, as shown:

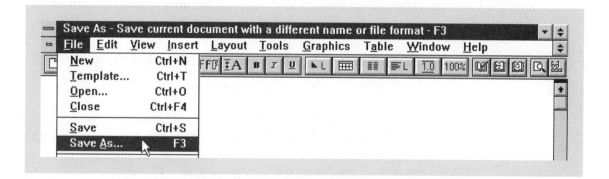

You'll see the same dialog box you saw the first time you saved this memo.

3. Click the down arrow in the Dri_ves_ box, and select the a: drive, as shown:

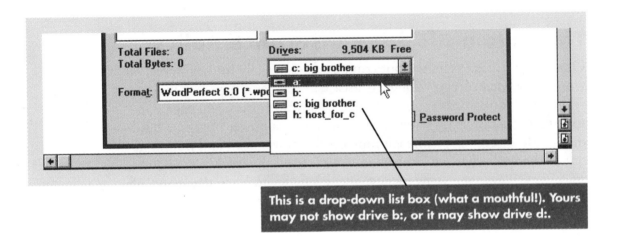

This is a drop-down list box (what a mouthful!). Yours may not show drive b:, or it may show drive d:.

● Note If your computer has two disk drives and you've put your disk in the second (lower or rightmost) drive, then you'll need to select the b: drive. It's okay if you select a:; you'll just see a warning dialog box in which WordPerfect will tell you that it can't read drive a: (because there's nothing in it). Don't let the words *System Error* scare you. Just click Cancel (twice, if necessary) and then select the b: drive.

4. Now click OK. (You could give the file a new name first, if you wanted to, but why bother?) WordPerfect saves your memo to the floppy disk.

WordPerfect has now forgotten about the first copy of your memo, which is all right—but you do have to be aware that, for instance, if you save the memo after making changes, you'll be saving the changes to the copy on the disk. (And if you've taken the disk out of the drive meanwhile, WordPerfect will get confused.) So remember to use Save As again, next time, instead of Save, and specify the c: drive again. (The c: drive is your hard disk. That's where the memo was saved originally.)

The Automatic Save Insurance Policy

One of the scariest things about computers, especially for beginners, is wondering what can go wrong. At least with pen and paper, or with a typewriter, your words are not going to just vanish from the page. Unfortunately, disasters do happen. Any disaster—a power outage, a hard-disk crash, or even someone tripping on the power cord and pulling it out of the wall—has the same effect. You lose all the work you've done, *since the last time you saved.* Believe me, it's better to learn the lesson of saving regularly the easy way, because if you don't, eventually you'll learn it the hard way.

Fortunately, WordPerfect provides you with a little insurance policy against disaster. It's called a *timed document backup.* What it does is save your work for you at regular intervals. You still have to save your document yourself, especially before quitting WordPerfect (see Lesson 5).

● Note If you do have a disaster at some point (knock wood), you just have to run WordPerfect again, and it will give you the chance to open the file and keep working on it, give it a name so you can find it later, or delete it.

Print the Easy Way

In some ways, printing is the most important feature of any word processor. What good is word wrap, editing, or computer memory if you can't get your work printed out on paper? As with most of its features, WordPerfect allows you all kinds of control over the printing process, but most of it is overkill, as usual. In this lesson I'll show you how to cut to the chase when it comes to printing, by taking advantage of one of WordPerfect's genuinely useful features, the Power Bar.

Two-Step Printing

The buttons on the Power Bar are all shortcuts. Each one of them stands for a command that you could select by pulling down the appropriate menu and choosing the proper option. Some are more useful than others. The Print button is one of the more useful ones because it saves you thumbing through the enormous File menu.

The buttons are *icons*, meaning that they show symbols instead of words. You're supposed to be able to look at any of them and tell what they mean. Don't feel stupid if they're not all crystal clear to you—that's the way it is with icons. Often they're obvious only to the programmers who designed them. The Print button is fourth from the left

Quick Easy

and has a little picture of a printer. Here, let me get my magnifying glass:

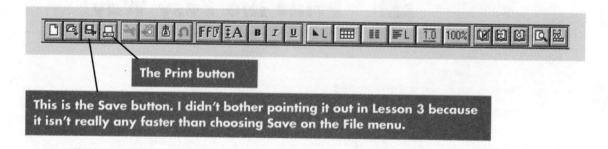

The Print button

This is the Save button. I didn't bother pointing it out in Lesson 3 because it isn't really any faster than choosing Save on the File menu.

To make a long story short (I know, I've been doing the opposite), here's the first step:

1. Click the Print button.

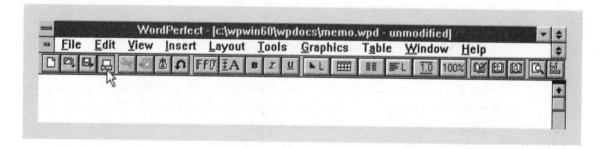

The following dialog box will appear:

Just click Print.

Ignore everything else.

2. Click Print.

Isn't that simple? Here's how the memo looks printed out on an HP LaserJet II:

MEMORANDUM
To: All Staff
From: Christian Crumlish
Date: June 11, 1994
Re: Four-day work week

As you all know, we have been experimenting for the past month with a four-day work week. I am pleased to announce that the preliminary results are in, and so far the experiment has been an amazing success. Productivity is off the scale!

I'm sure I'm not the only one here who used to dread Monday morning, but I think you'll all agree that it looks a lot brighter after a three-day weekend. Because of the success of our trial run, we are going to extend the four-day work week schedule for a further six months. If all goes well, and I don't see any reason why it shouldn't, we'll make the plan permanent.

The next experiment is telecommuting.

If your memo printed out okay, then you're done with this lesson. If you've run into a snag, there are a few easy things you can check.

No Fair! My Document Didn't Print Out!

If you followed my instruction but nothing came out of the printer, it could be a simple problem, easily fixed, or it might be something more complicated, in which case your best bet would be to call in your local guru to take a look. I'll tell you the simple things to check.

The most common problem in printing is that the printer is turned off or is *off line*, which means "not ready to print." Another potential source of the problem is that the cables that connect the printer to your computer are detached or have come loose. WordPerfect may or may not alert you to any of these problems.

Either way, here are some things to try:

- Make sure your printer is turned on. Every printer has an on/off switch somewhere prominent, so just look around and you'll see it.

- Make sure the printer is on line. Look for a button that says "Select," "ON LINE," or "Online/Offline." If there's a little message window, the message in it should be "Ready" or "Online," etc.

- Check that the cables into the printer are snug in their ports (sockets), both at the printer end and in the back of your computer.

- If it looks like the printer is turned on, on-line, and well connected to your computer, try turning the printer (not the computer!) off, wait a few seconds, and then turn it on again. You'd be amazed how often this simple trick gets things rolling again. (It's called "power cycling" if you're trying to impress someone with your jargon.)

- If you still can't tell what the problem is, you need the help of a guru who understands your setup.

5

When You Got to Go, You Got to Go

When you've finished what you're working on, or if you've had enough for one sitting, you can't just turn off your computer. First, you have to quit WordPerfect. This is very easy to do, so this lesson will be short.

Exiting Is Your Last Chance to Save

If you've been taking my advice so far, you've been saving your document whenever you make changes to it, and you've got nothing to worry about when it comes to losing your work. In case you forget, WordPerfect provides a safety net. When you try to leave the program, it checks to see if you've made any changes since the last time you saved, and if you have, it gives you one final chance to save your work before quitting.

Before the last time you saved the memo, you added a blank line at the end of it, as a token change. By the same token, delete that line now and then see what happens when you try to exit WordPerfect.

1. Press **PageDown** to make sure the insertion point is at the end of the document.

2. Press **Delete** once.

Quick & Easy

3. Pull down the <u>F</u>ile menu and select E<u>x</u>it, as shown:

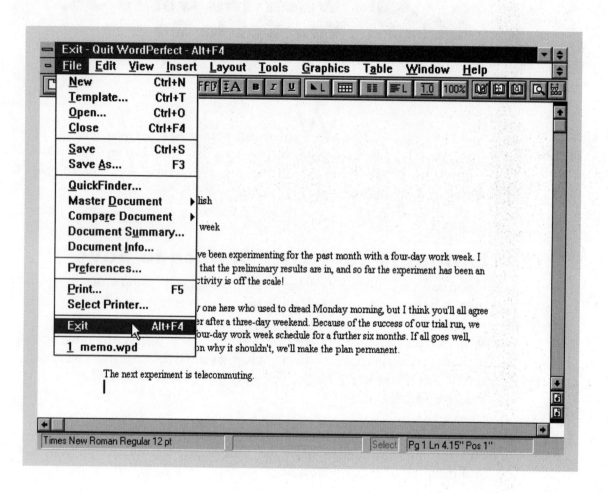

This dialog box appears:

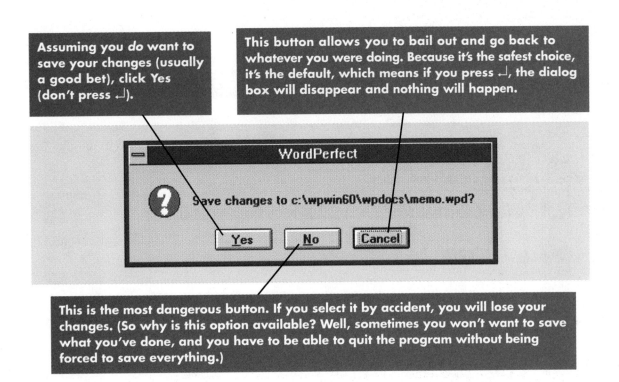

Assuming you *do* want to save your changes (usually a good bet), click Yes (don't press ↵).

This button allows you to bail out and go back to whatever you were doing. Because it's the safest choice, it's the default, which means if you press ↵, the dialog box will disappear and nothing will happen.

This is the most dangerous button. If you select it by accident, you will lose your changes. (So why is this option available? Well, sometimes you won't want to save what you've done, and you have to be able to quit the program without being forced to save everything.)

● **Note** If you are working on more than one document (something we'll discuss in Part Two), you'll be given this choice for each document with unsaved changes.

4. Click the Yes button.

If you have not previously saved your document (unlike memo.wpd), you will be taken to the Save As dialog box described in Lesson 3, and you can then give your document a name and save it. If your document already has a name (as is the case with memo.wpd), WordPerfect will save your most recent changes as soon as you click Yes.

After WordPerfect saves your changes, it shuts down and returns you to Windows.

You can quit Windows and return to DOS by pulling down the Program Manager's File menu and selecting Exit Windows. Click OK in the dialog box that appears.

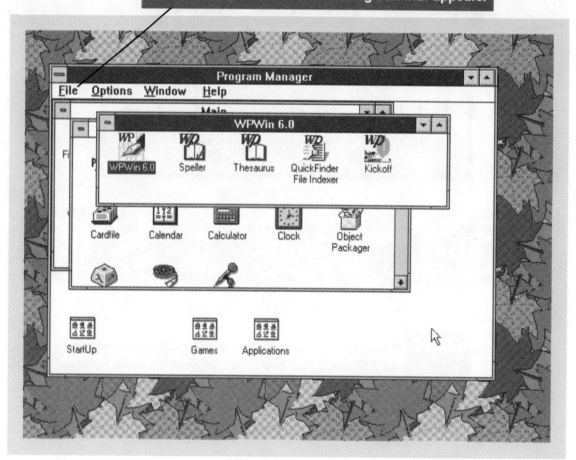

So that's what happens when you quit with unsaved changes. If you exit without having made any unsaved changes, no dialog box appears. WordPerfect just quits and returns you to Windows.

PART TWO

Get Things Into Shape

If you've worked your way through Part One, then you've written at least one simple document. You now know the basics of word processing with WordPerfect. In this part, I'll discuss the various ways you might want to improve the appearance of your document. You could get by just fine with what you already know, when it comes to getting words down on the page. But the usual purpose of writing is communication, and if you want people to read what you've written, it pays to shape up your document. I'll show you how to make some text stand out from the rest, how to control where the words appear on the page, and how to make a title page for a formal document. The first thing you'll learn is how to return to a document you've already written.

5 MINUTES

Pick Up
Where You Left Off

Okay, so you've written something. Your words are stored on your computer's disk. You have *hard copy*, meaning a copy of your document printed out on paper, but you realize that you'd like to fiddle around with it a little bit—see if you can make it look better. So where do you start? Well, the first thing you'll need to do is open up your document, that is to say, have WordPerfect find your document on the disk and display it on the screen so you can continue working with it. As soon as you successfully open your document, go on to the next lesson.

The Easy Way to Reopen Your Document

WordPerfect keeps track of the last four documents you (or anyone else) worked on. Unless a lot of water has gone under the bridge since the last time you saw your document, it will be listed for you at the bottom of the File menu. If you need to start WordPerfect and you forget how, refer to Lesson 1.

1. Pull down the File menu and select **memo.wpd**, as shown:

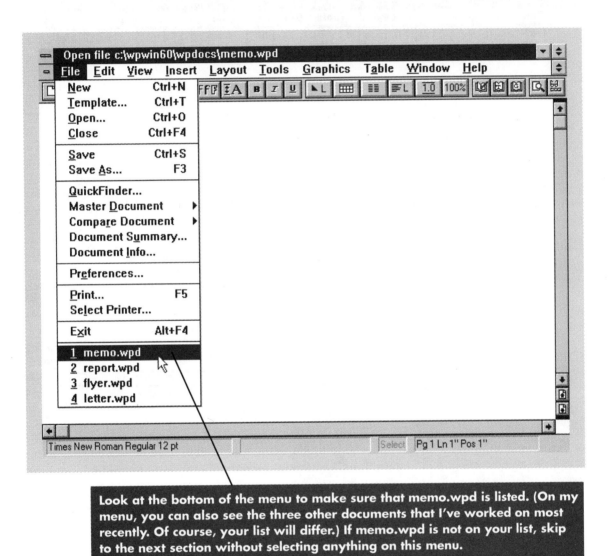

Look at the bottom of the menu to make sure that memo.wpd is listed. (On my menu, you can also see the three other documents that I've worked on most recently. Of course, your list will differ.) If memo.wpd is not on your list, skip to the next section without selecting anything on this menu.

WordPerfect retrieves your memo and displays it on the screen.

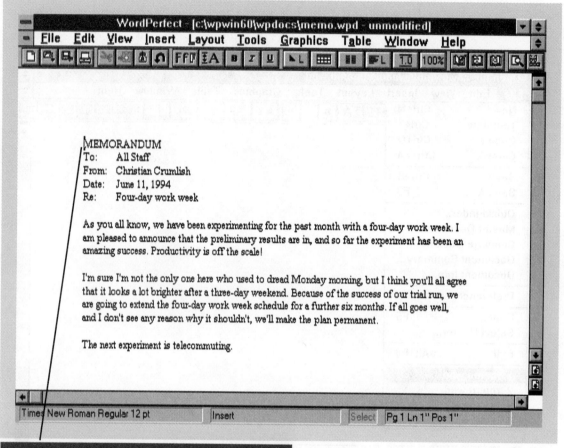

Notice that the insertion point is at the very beginning of the document (even if it was at the end when you last saved memo.wpd).

So that's the easy way. But even if your document has been replaced on the File menu by more recent ones, the steps for finding and retrieving it are pretty simple. (If you successfully opened memo.wpd just now, you can skip to the next lesson.)

Right Where You Left It

Whether or not you remember exactly where your document is, the procedure to open it is about the same:

1. Pull down the File menu and select Open, as shown:

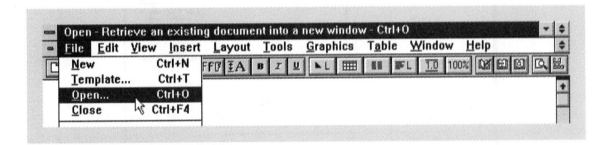

This dialog box will appear:

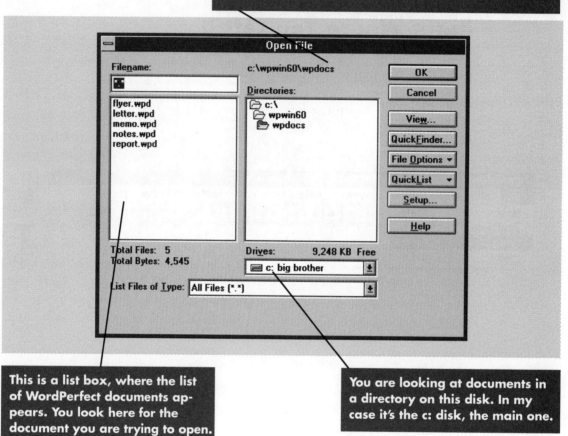

You are now looking at documents in this directory, wpdocs in the wpwin60 directory. This should be the directory to which you saved your document.

This is a list box, where the list of WordPerfect documents appears. You look here for the document you are trying to open.

You are looking at documents in a directory on this disk. In my case it's the c: disk, the main one.

● Note Déjà vu? This dialog box is very similar to the Save As dialog box you saw in Lesson 3.

2. If you see **memo.wpd** in the file list, double-click it, as shown:

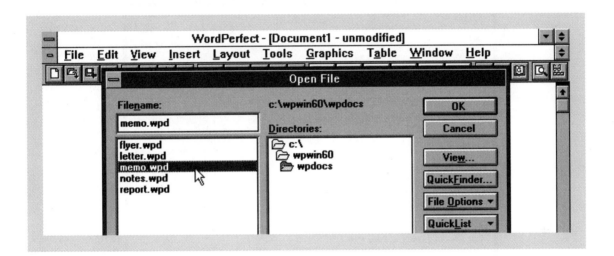

WordPerfect will retrieve your memo, and you're all set. If you did not see your document on the list, I'll help you find it.

What to Do If Your Document Is Hiding

If the list box is filled with the names of other documents, then the first thing you should try is scrolling the list.

1. Click below the scroll box in the little scroll bar at the right side of the list box, as shown:

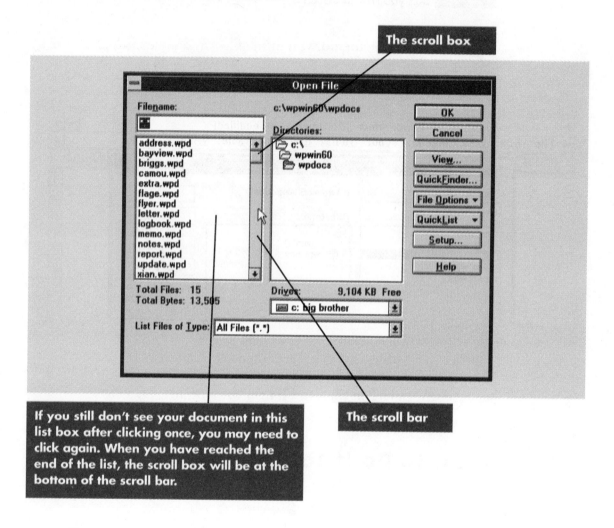

The scroll box

The scroll bar

If you still don't see your document in this list box after clicking once, you may need to click again. When you have reached the end of the list, the scroll box will be at the bottom of the scroll bar.

2. As you reveal the rest of the list, continue looking for **memo.wpd**. If you see it, double-click on it.

If you still don't see it, that means your current directory (the one shown under Directories to the right of the list box) must not be wpdocs. (Remember, you saved the memo to the wpdocs directory in Lesson 3.)

3. Double-click on **wpdocs** in the Directories list box, as
shown:

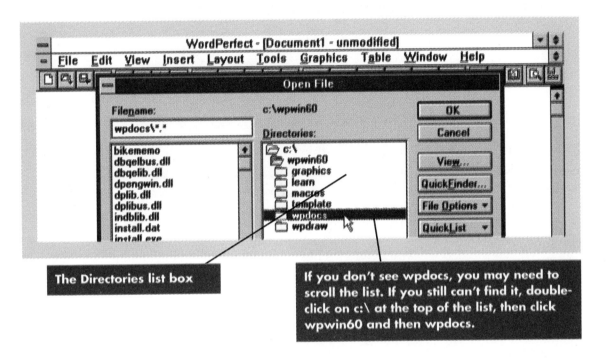

The Directories list box

If you don't see wpdocs, you may need to
scroll the list. If you still can't find it, double-
click on c:\ at the top of the list, then click
wpwin60 and then wpdocs.

4. Look through the list for **memo.wpd** and double-click on it.

Start Something New

So now you've got memo.wpd on the screen. You've learned how to return to something where you left off. But what do you do if you want to work on something new? Remember, to write your first document you just started typing—the screen was blank. But now, imagine you've finished working on one document, one project, whatever, and you want to start some other project. You can start a new document without getting rid of the old one. In this lesson I'll show you how.

The Easiest Way to Start a New Document

You'll like this. It's just one step:

1. Click the leftmost icon on the Power Bar, as shown:

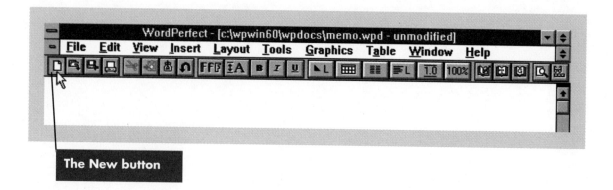

The New button

• Note There is a New command on the File menu, but it's so easy to just click the leftmost button on the Power Bar that you'll be doing it without thinking soon.

Instantly, WordPerfect starts a new document for you and the typing area is cleared.

In the title bar, your new document is called Document2. If you start another new one now, it would be called Document3, and so on.

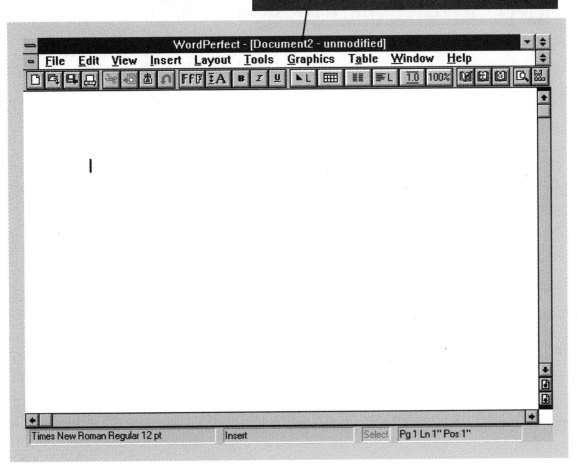

You're ready to begin typing a new document.

What Happened to My First Document?

You may now be wondering what happened to memo.wpd. Don't worry. It's still there—you just can't see it right now. Try this:

1. Pull down the <u>W</u>indow menu (second from the right) and select memo.wpd, like so:

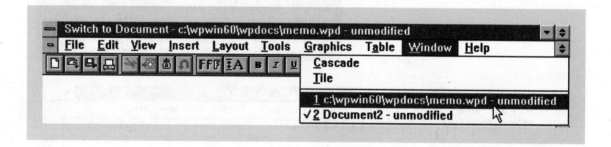

Look familiar? It works both ways.

2. Pull down the <u>W</u>indow menu and select **Document 2 – unmodified**.

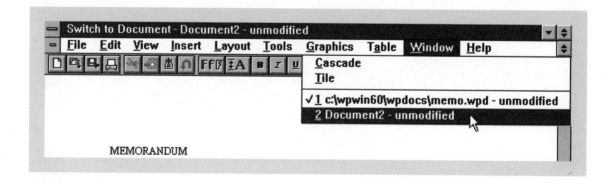

That's all there is to switching between open documents.

A Larger Sample Document

In the rest of Part Two, you will learn how to emphasize text and control the appearance of your pages. You probably won't need to fiddle much with short documents like the memo you typed. That's why I'd like you to have a longer document to work with, in fact one that covers several pages. A report is a typical example. Of course, I don't expect you to type pages and pages of my entertaining prose, so I'll give you a little bit to begin with and then we'll fake the rest.

1. Type this title, subtitle, and a name (yours, mine, or a made-up one):

Midday Siestas and Workers' Productivity ⏎

A Proposal ⏎

Christian Crumlish ⏎

Department of Human Resources ⏎

2. Now, press ⏎ twice to skip two lines.

Midday Siestas and Workers' Productivity
A Proposal
Christian Crumlish
Department of Human Resources

3. Type the following report opener (remember, don't press ↵
until you get to the end of the paragraph):

In many of the more southerly countries it is well known that a person
can get more work done and enjoy more of work, and indeed of life,
simply by taking a nap in the middle of the day. In Spanish speaking
countries this is known as a siesta. There's more than one way to divide up eight hours. ↵

Now you need a dummy paragraph to fill out the rest of the report.

4. Press ↵ to insert a blank line.

5. Type this paragraph (I promise this is the last one):

The words in this paragraph are all filler. Repeated many times, they
will give the appearance of a full-length document. On and on the
paragraph rambles, drifting further and further into random sounding
strings of words. Of course, it doesn't really have to say anything. As
long as it looks like a typical paragraph, it will do. Another sentence
or two and it will be long enough. Just one more and it will be perfect! There, that ought to do it. ↵

● Note To build this large document, I'm going to ask you to do some
things without much explanation. I'll explain more about things
like copying and pasting in Part Three. But first things first.

Your screen should look something like this:

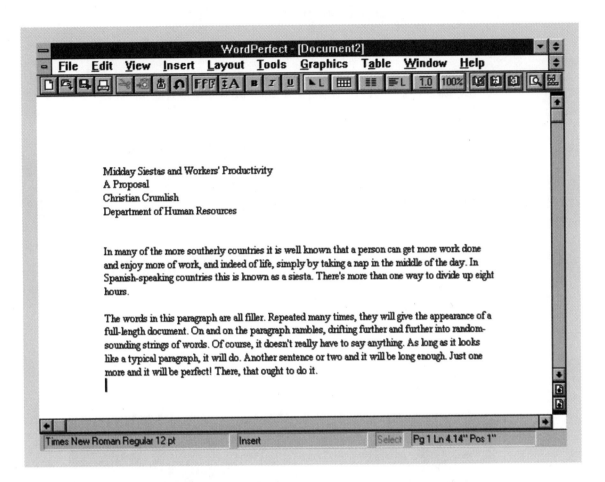

I'm sure that's enough typing for you. To avoid typing all day, you're going to copy this paragraph a bunch of times to give the appearance of a longer document.

6. Hit ↵ one more time.

7. Press ↑ six times, so the insertion point is to the left of the T in *The* at the beginning of the paragraph.

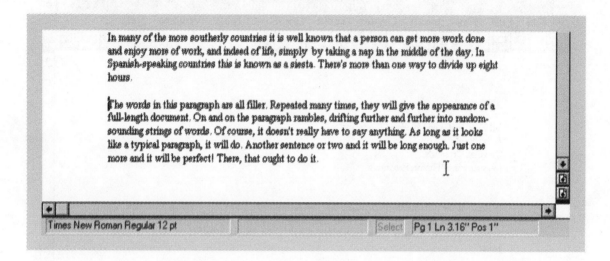

8. Hold down **Shift** and press **PageDown**. The entire paragraph is selected, as is the blank line at the end.

9. Click the sixth button on the Power Bar, the one that looks like a clipboard (between the scissors and the paste pot).

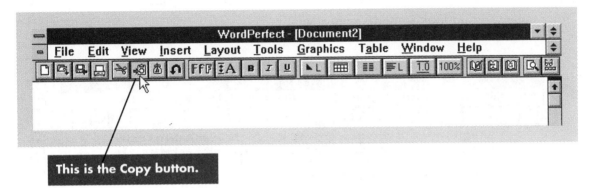

This is the Copy button.

10. Hit PageDown.

11. Now click the next button to the right, the one with the paste pot on it.

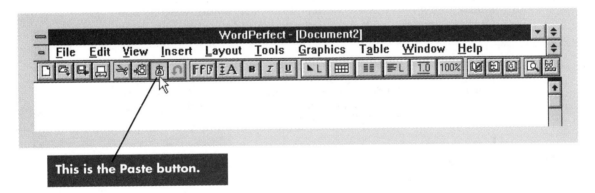

This is the Paste button.

The dummy paragraph is copied once.

12. Click the Paste button 16 times (or so); the dummy paragraph is repeated over and over.

Your screen should look something like this:

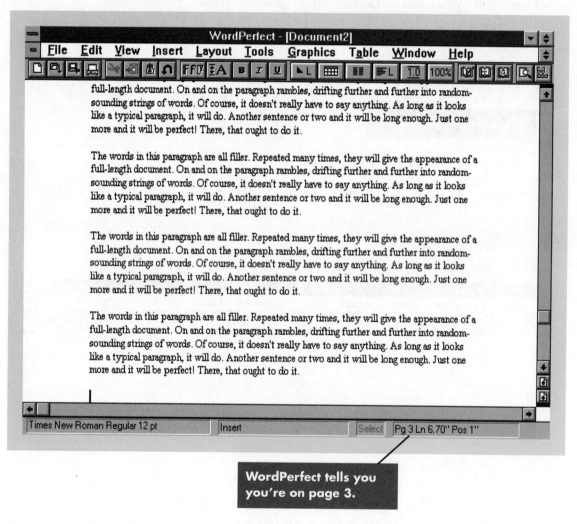

WordPerfect tells you you're on page 3.

So now you have a long document. Save it as **siesta** in the **wpdocs** directory. (Refer to Lesson 3 if you need a reminder about how to save.)

Find Your Way Around

With a long document, such as SIESTA, which you just created in Lesson 7, you can see only part of it on the screen at any time. So there are a few things you ought to know about getting from one part of a document to another. In this lesson I'll show you how to move the insertion point anywhere you want and how to scroll through a document. If you've exited since the last lesson, open SIESTA before continuing. You learned to open a document in Lesson 6..

Giant Steps

You've already picked up some of the common ways to move the insertion point. One way is to position the I-beam and click. Another is to press the arrow keys, such as ↑ and →.

It's not always convenient to use the mouse to get around. Sometimes you'd rather keep your hands close to the keyboard. But it gets mighty tedious hitting → five hundred times to get to the next page. There are shortcuts. Try some now.

1. Press **Ctrl+Home**. The insertion point jumps to the beginning of the document.

Quick Easy

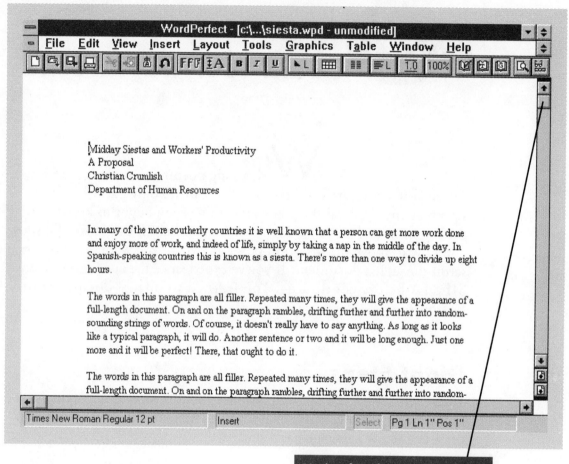

Notice that the scroll box is at
the top of the scroll bar.

● Note If you've just reopened SIESTA, the insertion point is already at
the beginning of the document, so nothing will happen when
you hit **Ctrl+Home**.

2. Press **Ctrl+End**. The insertion point jumps back to the end
of the document.

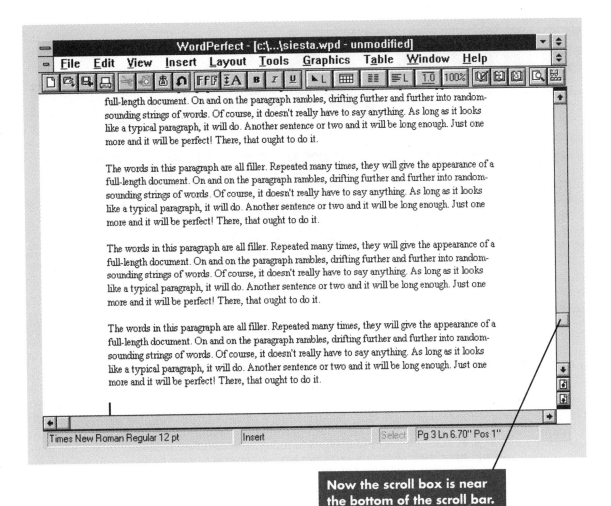

The words in this paragraph are all filler. Repeated many times, they will give the appearance of a full-length document. On and on the paragraph rambles, drifting further and further into random-sounding strings of words. Of course, it doesn't really have to say anything. As long as it looks like a typical paragraph, it will do. Another sentence or two and it will be long enough. Just one more and it will be perfect! There, that ought to do it.

Now the scroll box is near the bottom of the scroll bar.

3. Press **PageUp**. The insertion point jumps to the top of the screen.

4. Press **PageUp** again. Your view has jumped up one window—one screenful of text—above your previous view and the insertion point is still at the top of the screen.

Quick&Easy

You've moved up one window and the insertion
point is still at the top of the screen.

The edges, shadow, and gray background represent
the end of page 2 and the beginning of page 3.

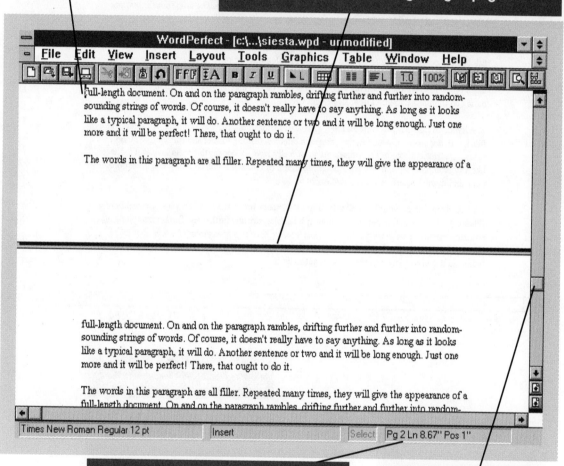

This shows that the insertion point is on
page 2 (it's above the page break).

The location of the scroll
box in the scroll bar
gives you some idea of
where you are now in
the document (near but
not quite *at* the end).

● **Note** Don't worry if your screen doesn't match mine exactly. What's important is noticing how the screen moves.

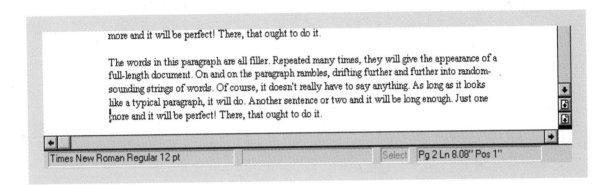

5. Press End. The insertion point jumps to the end of the line.

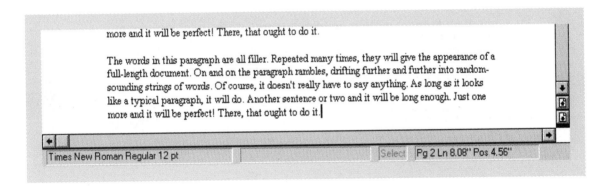

6. Press Home. The insertion point returns to the beginning of the line.

Those are the ways to make big jumps around your document. Now, slightly smaller steps.

One Step at a Time

You won't always want to skip to the end of your document or even all the way to the end of the line. Sometimes you'll be aiming for the middle of a line, say, or for a point just a few paragraphs down.

1. Press →. The insertion point moves to the right one character.

2. Now press Ctrl+→. This time the insertion point moves to the beginning of the next word.

3. Press Ctrl+→ again. The insertion point moves one more word to the right.

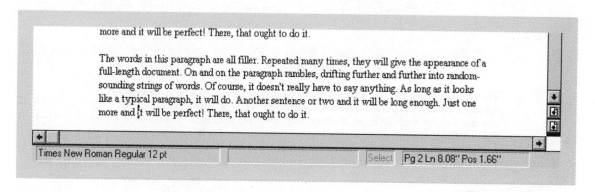

more and it will be perfect! There, that ought to do it.

The words in this paragraph are all filler. Repeated many times, they will give the appearance of a full-length document. On and on the paragraph rambles, drifting further and further into random-sounding strings of words. Of course, it doesn't really have to say anything. As long as it looks like a typical paragraph, it will do. Another sentence or two and it will be long enough. Just one more and it will be perfect! There, that ought to do it.

Times New Roman Regular 12 pt   Select Pg 2 Ln 8.08" Pos 1.66"

4. Press End. The insertion point moves to the end of the line.

5. Press ←. The insertion point moves to the left one character.

6. Press Ctrl+←. The insertion point moves to the beginning of the word it's on.

7. Press **Ctrl**+← again. The insertion point moves one word to the left.

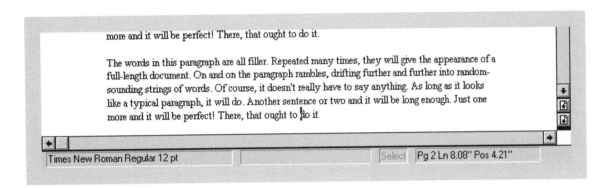

You can see that using **Ctrl** with ← and → is a good way to skip quickly through a line. The **Ctrl** key has a similar "exaggerating" effect on ↑ and ↓.

8. Press **Home**.

9. Press ↑. The insertion point moves up one line of text.

10. Press **Ctrl**+↑. The insertion point moves to the beginning of the paragraph.

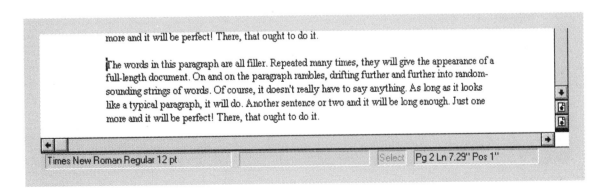

11. Press ↓. The insertion point moves down one line of text.

12. Press Ctrl+↓. The insertion point moves down to the beginning of the next paragraph.

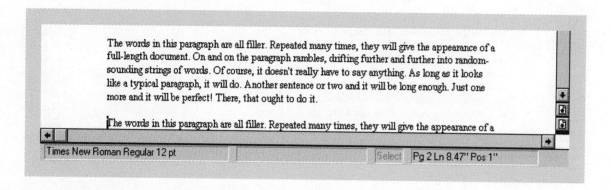

The words in this paragraph are all filler. Repeated many times, they will give the appearance of a full-length document. On and on the paragraph rambles, drifting further and further into random-sounding strings of words. Of course, it doesn't really have to say anything. As long as it looks like a typical paragraph, it will do. Another sentence or two and it will be long enough. Just one more and it will be perfect! There, that ought to do it.

The words in this paragraph are all filler. Repeated many times, they will give the appearance of a

Times New Roman Regular 12 pt   Select   Pg 2 Ln 8.47" Pos 1"

Finally, I'll show you a few ways to move to another part of the document without moving the insertion point.

Scrolling, Scrolling, Scrolling

There will be times when you'll need to look at another part of your document and then return to exactly where you left off. At such times, you might as well leave the insertion point where it is and just *scroll* to the area you want to look at.

There are three ways to scroll. Try the first way now.

1. Move the mouse pointer to the vertical scroll bar, above the scroll box, and click once. (Don't hold down the mouse button.)

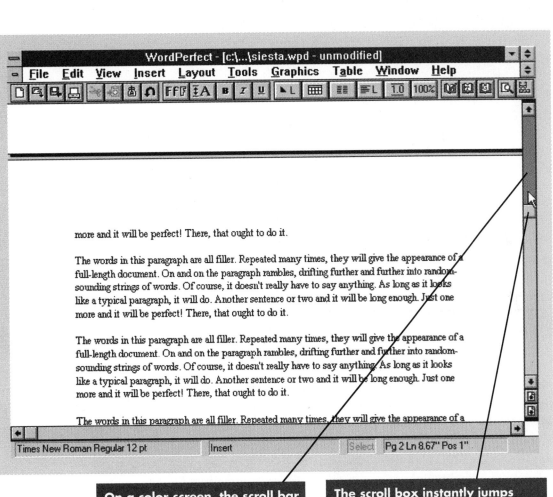

On a color screen, the scroll bar darkens when you click it.

The scroll box instantly jumps upward, to give you a sense of where you are in your document.

• Note You may never even need to use the horizontal scroll bar at the bottom of the screen. It is for viewing text that is too wide to fit in the window.

Your view of the text "scrolls" upward, showing the screenful of text just above the one you were looking at before. (Notice that the insertion point is no longer on the screen.) This procedure is the same one

you've already used to scroll through list boxes when saving or opening documents.

Here is the second way to scroll:

2. Click the downward pointing scroll arrow at the bottom end of the vertical scroll bar (above the two buttons with dog-eared pages on them).

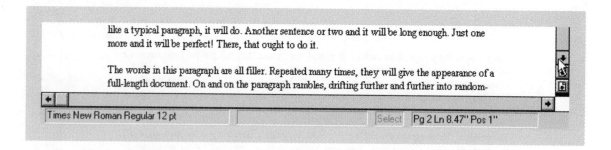

The view scrolls a bit down the page, but not enough to bring the insertion point back onto the screen (and the scroll bar shifts slightly lower). Use the scroll arrow when you don't want to jump whole screenfuls at a time.

The final way to scroll allows you the most control:

3. Click the scroll box and drag it to the top of the scroll bar.

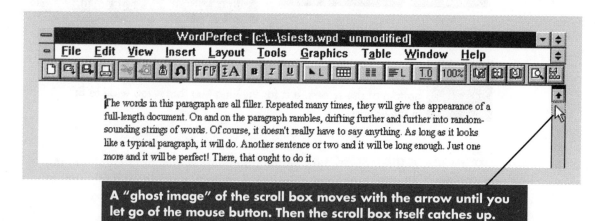

A "ghost image" of the scroll box moves with the arrow until you let go of the mouse button. Then the scroll box itself catches up.

As soon as you release the mouse button, the document scrolls to the top. When you want to see a part of the document somewhere in the middle, drag the scroll box to a position roughly the same fraction of the scroll bar. (For instance, if you want to see a part of the document about a third of the way into it, drag the scroll box about a third of the way down the scroll bar.)

Look around the screen and you won't see the insertion point. It's still where you left it before you started scrolling around.

4. Press **Ctrl+Home** to bring the insertion point to the beginning of the document.

● Note The other two buttons at the bottom of the vertical scroll bar will scroll your view one page at a time, up or down. (That's real pages as printed, not screenfuls.)

Now you know the ins and outs of finding your way around a long document, and you're ready to learn how to improve the appearance of your document.

5 MINUTES

LESSON 9

Enhance Your Text for Emphasis

So far you've been making plain-vanilla documents. All the text looks the same. Sometimes you'll want to draw attention to a specific word or phrase or even section of your document. Sometimes clear communication requires emphasis. In this lesson I'll show you how to select the text you want to emphasize and then how to make the text **bold**, *italicized,* or <u>underlined</u>. You should have siesta.wpd on your screen.

Select the Text You Want to Affect

The basic way to select text is to click at one end of the selection and (without letting up the mouse button) drag to the other end of the selection. Try this now:

1. Position the I-beam just before the word *indeed* on the second line of the first paragraph, click, and hold down the mouse button.

2. Drag the I-beam to the end of the word *paragraph* on the first line of the second paragraph and release the mouse button. The selected text is reversed on a black background.

62

In many of the more southerly countries it is well known that a person can get more work done and enjoy more of work, and indeed of life, simply by taking a nap in the middle of the day. In Spanish-speaking countries this is known as a siesta. There's more than one way to divide up eight hours.

The words in this paragraph are all filler. Repeated many times, they will give the appearance of a full-length document. On and on the paragraph rambles, drifting further and further into random-

Notice that the blank line between the paragraphs is also part of the selection.

There are a few slicker shortcuts you might want to know about as well. For instance, you can select a single word.

3. Double-click on the word *indeed.* It is selected.

Department of Human Resources

In many of the more southerly countries it is well known that a person can get more work done and enjoy more of work, and indeed of life, simply by taking a nap in the middle of the day. In Spanish-speaking countries this is known as a siesta. There's more than one way to divide up eight hours.

When you select a word, the space immediately after the word is also part of the selection.

You can select an entire sentence.

4. Triple-click on the word *countries.* The sentence it is in is selected.

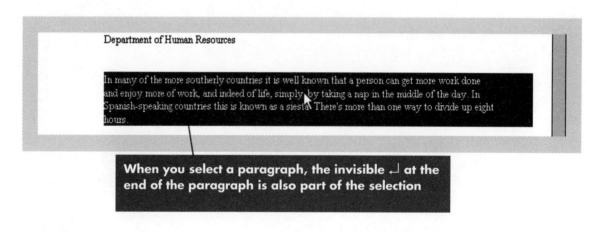

Department of Human Resources

In many of the more southerly countries it is well known that a person can get more work done and enjoy more of work, and indeed of life, simply by taking a nap in the middle of the day. In Spanish-speaking countries this is known as a siesta. There's more than one way to divide up eight hours.

When you select a sentence, the space immediately after the sentence is also part of the selection.

You can also select a whole paragraph:

5. Quadruple-click on the word *simply*. The entire paragraph is selected.

Department of Human Resources

In many of the more southerly countries it is well known that a person can get more work done and enjoy more of work, and indeed of life, simply by taking a nap in the middle of the day. In Spanish-speaking countries this is known as a siesta. There's more than one way to divide up eight hours.

When you select a paragraph, the invisible ⏎ at the end of the paragraph is also part of the selection

● Note If you click the wrong number of times, just start over and try again. You'll get it.

And, wouldn't you know it, you can select the entire document.

1. Put the mouse pointer in the left margin of the document.

2. Click the *right* mouse button. This will produce a pop-up menu right where the mouse pointer is.

3. Choose Select All.

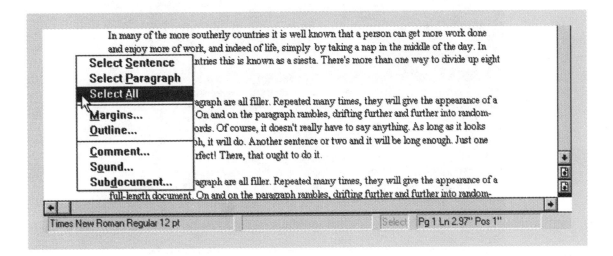

The entire document will be selected.

• Note It's dangerous to keep the whole document selected for very long. It's too easy to delete the whole thing, for example.

Quick & Easy

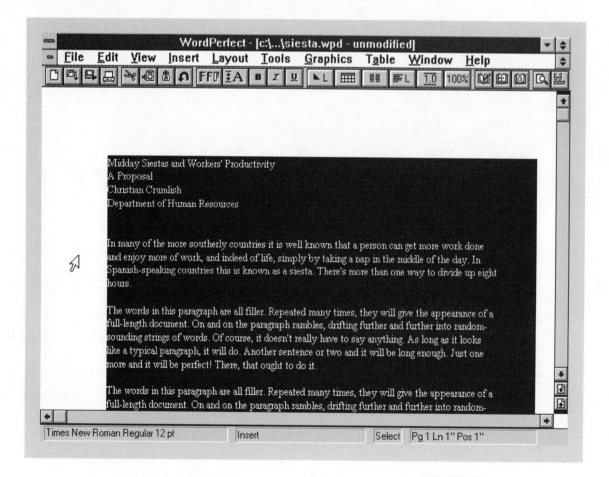

4. Now click somewhere else.

Now on to the fun stuff.

To Boldly Go...

Select text, then emphasize—that's the routine. The most common types of emphasis are available on the Power Bar, as shown:

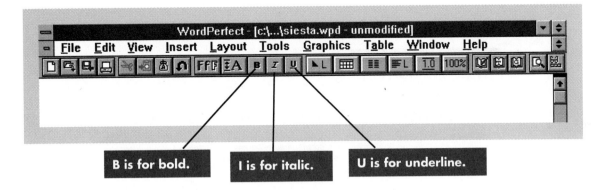

Now, boldface the title of the report.

1. Select (triple-click) the first line of the report.

2. Click the Bold button, as shown. The line is boldfaced.

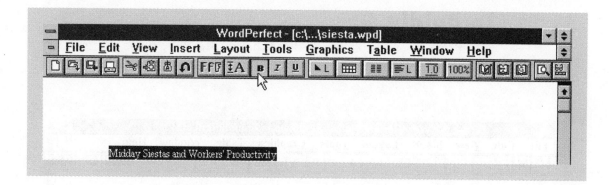

3. Click on another line to see the bold line more clearly.

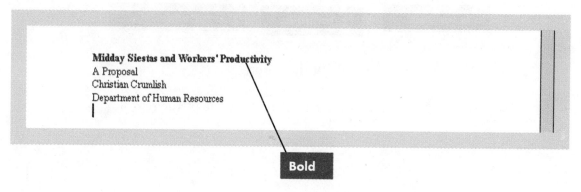

Bold

Now, try out the other two buttons:

4. Select the fourth line, **Department of Human Resources**.

5. Click the Underline button.

6. Select the word *siesta* (double-click) in the third line of the first paragraph.

7. Click the Italic button.

> **Midday Siestas and Workers' Productivity**
> A Proposal
> Christian Crumlish
> <u>Department of Human Resources</u>
>
> In many of the more southerly countries it is well known that a person can get more work done and enjoy more of work, and indeed of life, simply by taking a nap in the middle of the day. In Spanish-speaking countries this is known as a *siesta*. There's more than one way to divide up eight hours.

Underlined

Italic

• Note You can combine any and all forms of emphasis. You can make text bold *and* italic. You can underline one bold word in a bold sentence. But wait, there's more.

Emphasis On the Fly

If you know ahead of time that you want to emphasize some text, you can click the appropriate button first, and *then* type the text.

1. Click between the word *anything* and the period that follows it, in the middle of the second paragraph. The insertion point will appear there.

2. Type a space.

3. Click the Italic button.

4. Type **at all**. (Don't type the period—it's one of mine.)

The Italic button remains pressed as you type.

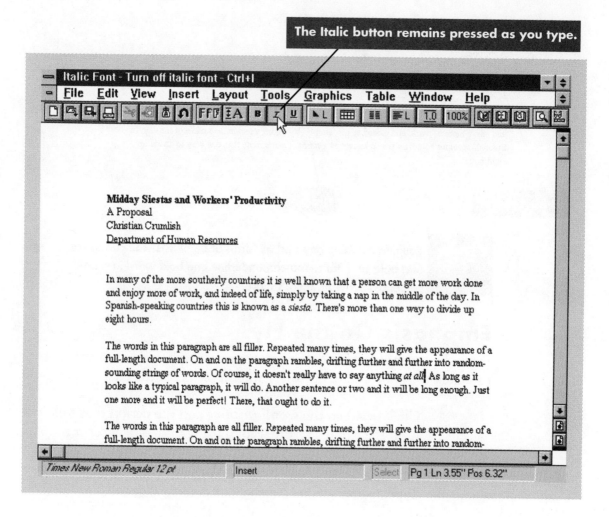

5. Click the Italic button again. It no longer appears to be pressed down.

• Note Get into the habit of unpressing buttons when you are finished using them. It's sometimes inconvenient when you forget to.

You can remove emphasis just as easily. If you change your mind or want to remove emphasis you've added by mistake, just select the text and click the button so it's *not* pressed down. The emphasis will be removed.

That's all you need to know about emphasis. There *are* other ways to improve the appearance of your words. In the next lesson, I'll show you how to change the size and the style of text.

5 MINUTES

Change Font and Size

10

A s I mentioned at the end of the previous lesson, there are still other ways to vary or improve the appearance of your text. We'll continue to use the SIESTA report as a guinea pig as I show you how to change two things—*font* and *size*. Font means type style; size you know.

Use Different Fonts for Different Occasions

Some fonts are formal and look authoritative. Others are more casual and relaxed. Some are easier to read than others. Others make good, attention-grabbing headlines. Windows comes with a basic set of fonts and WordPerfect comes with a bunch more, so you are provided with some variety.

The first thing to do is select the text whose font you want to change.

1. Select the first line of the report title.

> Midday Siestas and Workers' Productivity
> A Proposal
> Christian Crumlish
> Department of Human Resources

● **Note** Lesson 9 explains how to select text.

2. Click the button on the Power Bar with three *f*s on it (the Font Face button), as shown:

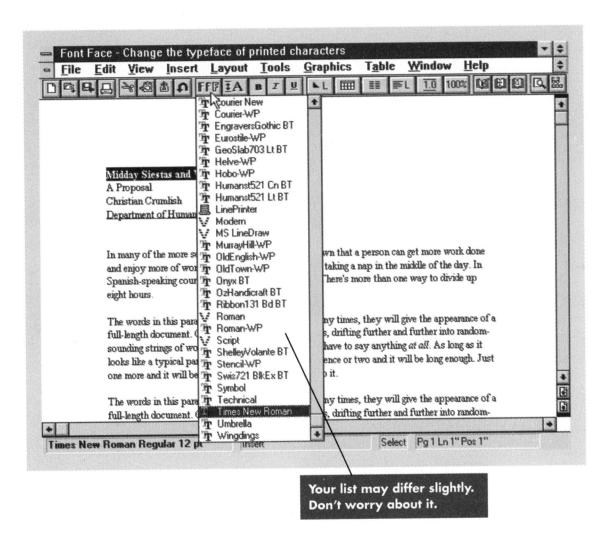

Font Face - Change the typeface of printed characters

File   Edit   View   Insert   Layout   Tools   Graphics   Table   Window   Help

Courier New
Courier-WP
EngraversGothic BT
Eurostile-WP
GeoSlab703 Lt BT
Helve-WP
Hobo-WP
Humanst521 Cn BT
Humanst521 Lt BT
LinePrinter
Modern
MS LineDraw
MurrayHill-WP
OldEnglish-WP
OldTown-WP
Onyx BT
OzHandicraft BT
Ribbon131 Bd BT
Roman
Roman-WP
Script
ShelleyVolante BT
Stencil-WP
Swis721 BlkEx BT
Symbol
Technical
Times New Roman
Umbrella
Wingdings

Midday Siestas and
A Proposal
Christian Crumlish
Department of Human

In many of the more s
and enjoy more of wor
Spanish-speaking cour
eight hours.

The words in this para
full-length document.
sounding strings of wo
looks like a typical pa
one more and it will be

The words in this para
full-length document.

wn that a person can get more work done
taking a nap in the middle of the day. In
here's more than one way to divide up

my times, they will give the appearance of a
s, drifting further and further into random-
have to say anything *at all*. As long as it
ence or two and it will be long enough. Just
o it.

my times, they will give the appearance of a
s, drifting further and further into random-

Times New Roman Regular 12 p   insert   Select   Pg 1 Ln 1" Pos 1"

Your list may differ slightly. Don't worry about it.

3. Scroll to the top of the list and click on the word **Arial**. The list box disappears as soon as you release the mouse button.

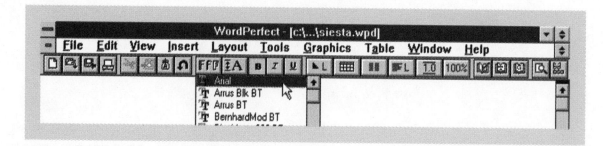

4. Click anywhere to see the change more clearly.

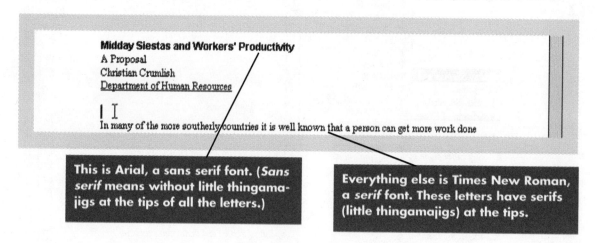

This is Arial, a sans serif font. (*Sans serif* means without little thingamajigs at the tips of all the letters.)

Everything else is Times New Roman, a *serif* font. These letters have serifs (little thingamajigs) at the tips.

It's that easy to change fonts. Experiment sometime with the fonts you have available, just so you know what you've got. You can also change to a new font and *then* type your text in that font.

Now let's try some different sizes.

One Size Doesn't Fit All

Changing the size of your text is as easy as changing the font. Follow these instructions to make the report's title text bigger. The first line is the title itself, so it needs to be the largest.

1. Select the title of the report.

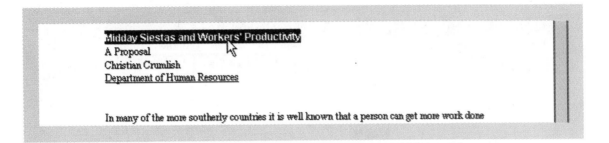

2. Click the button on the Power Bar with the letter *A* on it (the Font Size button), to the right of the Font Face button, as shown:

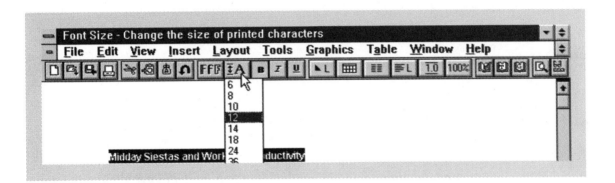

• Note Text size is measured in units called *points*. Everything you've typed so far has been 12-point text. Typewriters make letters between 10 and 12 points (about one-sixth of an inch).

We don't want to make the title *too* big.

3. Click **18**.

Quick ♦ Easy

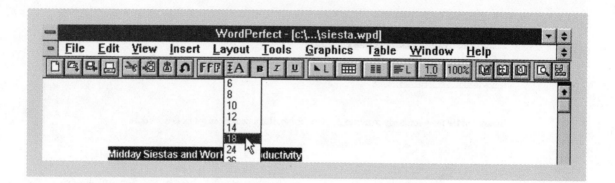

4. Click anywhere to see the result.

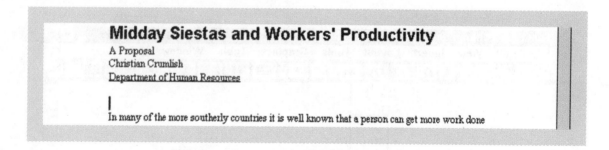

Now the next three lines look too small. Let's set their point size to 14.

5. Select the next three lines.

6. Click the Font Size button again.

7. Click **14**.

8. Click somewhere else.

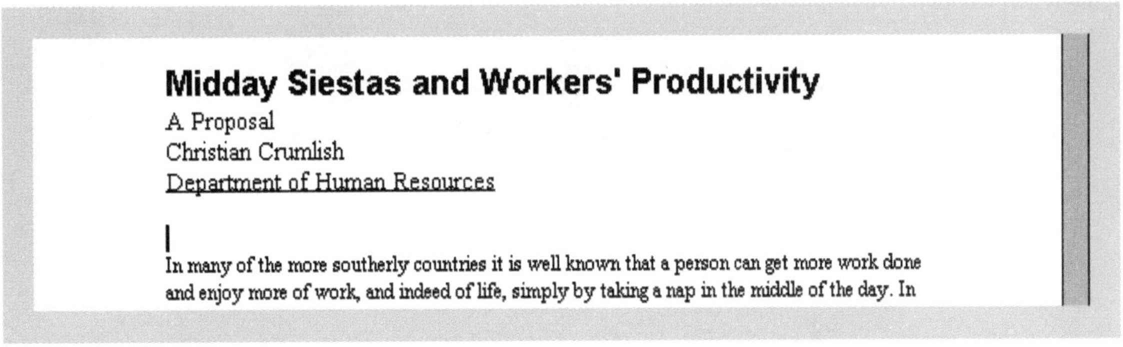

Midday Siestas and Workers' Productivity

A Proposal
Christian Crumlish
Department of Human Resources

In many of the more southerly countries it is well known that a person can get more work done
and enjoy more of work, and indeed of life, simply by taking a nap in the middle of the day. In

There, now doesn't that look imposing and authoritative? Just as with fonts and many other WordPerfect features, you can always set a new size and *then* type the text you want in that size.

In the next lesson, I'll show you how to center text or otherwise change its alignment.

5 MINUTES

Position Text on the Page

11

Look at your document. Notice how all the words line up along the left edge and how they're uneven at the right edge? This is called *left alignment*, or *ragged right*. It's the way typewritten words look. Maybe you like the way it looks just fine. Most of the time it will do. But there are a few other options. Let's try some of them now with the SIESTA report.

Take Center Stage

Turn your attention once again to the Power Bar. Look for the button with the letter *L* on it next to some lines:

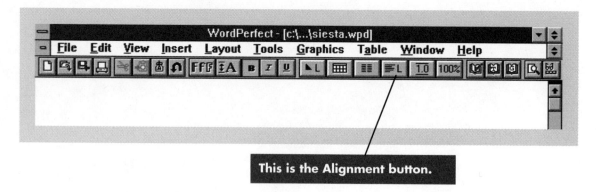

This is the Alignment button.

Let's center the title and subtitle:

1. Select the first two lines.

2. Click the Alignment button (hold down the mouse button).

3. Select Center, as shown:

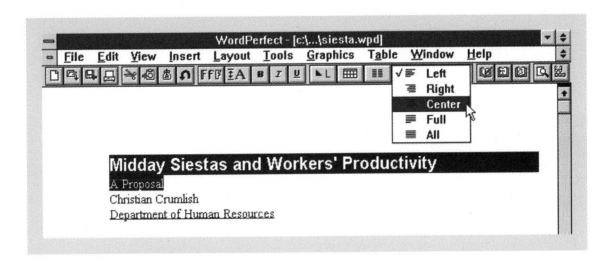

4. Click anywhere. Your title and subtitle should look like this:

Let's give the title a little breathing room:

5. Click just to the left of the report author's name, so the insertion point is before the first letter.

> **Midday Siestas and Workers' Productivity**
> A Proposal
>
> Christian Crumlish
> Department of Human Resources

● Note If you click too far to the left, you'll select the whole line. Just click again until you get it right.

6. Press ↵.

> **Midday Siestas and Workers' Productivity**
> A Proposal
>
> Christian Crumlish
> Department of Human Resources

Here is the blank line you just entered.

On the Right Side

Now let's move the name and department to the right:

1. Select the name and the underlined department name.

2. Click the Alignment button.

3. Select Right, as shown:

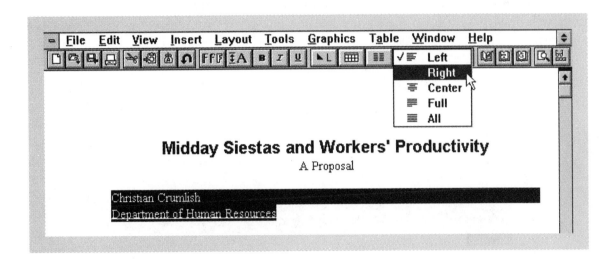

4. Click somewhere else. Your screen should look like this.

What could be easier?

Justification in Time

There's one other alignment you need to see in action. It aligns the text at the left *and* the right. How does it do this? Well, it spaces out the words as necessary so that all lines are the same length (except the last lines of paragraphs). Many books have this sort of alignment, which is

Quick **Easy**

also called *full justification.* It makes words look more formal, more "published." While it may not be appropriate for something simple like a memo, it's just the thing for a report. (Also, the words below the name will line up with it on the right edge.) So let's try it on the first paragraph.

1. Select the first paragraph by quadruple-clicking on it, as shown:

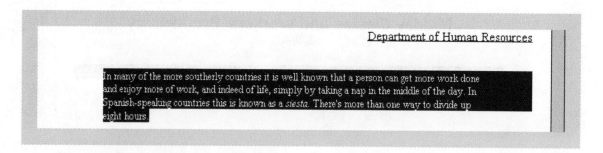

2. Click the Alignment button.

3. Select Full, as shown:

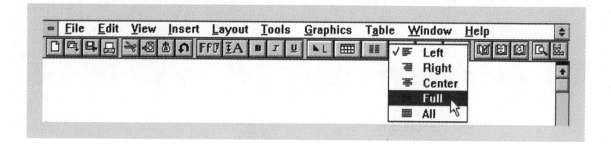

The paragraph is now fully justified:

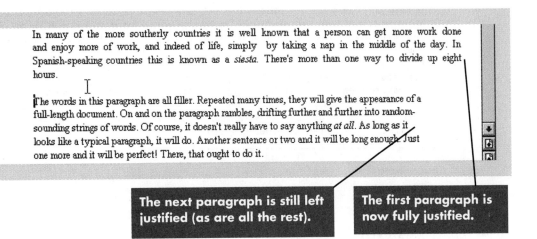

In many of the more southerly countries it is well known that a person can get more work done and enjoy more of work, and indeed of life, simply by taking a nap in the middle of the day. In Spanish-speaking countries this is known as a *siesta*. There's more than one way to divide up eight hours.

The words in this paragraph are all filler. Repeated many times, they will give the appearance of a full-length document. On and on the paragraph rambles, drifting further and further into random-sounding strings of words. Of course, it doesn't really have to say anything *at all*. As long as it looks like a typical paragraph, it will do. Another sentence or two and it will be long enough. Just one more and it will be perfect! There, that ought to do it.

The next paragraph is still left justified (as are all the rest).

The first paragraph is now fully justified.

To assign something like alignment from any point in the document all the way to the end, just put the insertion point where you want the new alignment to start, but don't select any text. Then choose the alignment you want.

1. Place the I-beam just before the next paragraph.

2. Click the Alignment button and select Full.

The rest of the report is now fully justified.

In many of the more southerly countries it is well known that a person can get more work done and enjoy more of work, and indeed of life, simply by taking a nap in the middle of the day. In Spanish-speaking countries this is known as a *siesta*. There's more than one way to divide up eight hours.

The words in this paragraph are all filler. Repeated many times, they will give the appearance of a full-length document. On and on the paragraph rambles, drifting further and further into random-sounding strings of words. Of course, it doesn't really have to say anything *at all*. As long as it looks like a typical paragraph, it will do. Another sentence or two and it will be long enough. Just one more and it will be perfect! There, that ought to do it.

Times New Roman Regular 12 pt

Select   Pg 1 Ln 3.37" Pos 1"

3. Press Ctrl+Home to get back to the top of the report.

So now you know how to put the words wherever you want on the page.

12

Paragraph Indents the Quick Way

By now you may realize that WordPerfect separates the two jobs of typing and formatting. When you are trying to write something, you should not have to be thinking about how it's going to look. You just want to type in your words. Later, you can go back and fix up their appearance. In the last lesson I showed you how to change alignment. In this lesson and the next few, I'll show you other easy formatting tricks.

Setting a Paragraph Indent

In both sample documents I've asked you to type, each paragraph begins with no indent. Each one is flush with the left margin. This is the best way to type even if you'd like your paragraphs to start with an indent. There's no point in typing spaces or tabs before the first word of *every* paragraph. In some cases that will even end up inconveniencing you.

Fortunately, there is a way to indent one or all of your paragraphs after you've finished typing them. I'll show you how to do this now.

1. Put the insertion point just before the first letter in the first paragraph *(I)*, as shown:

> Christian Crumlish
> Department of Human Resources

> In many of the more southerly countries it is well known that a person can get more work done and enjoy more of work, and indeed of life, simply by taking a nap in the middle of the day. In Spanish-speaking countries this is known as a *siesta*. There's more than one way to divide up eight hours.

2. Pull down the Layout menu, select Paragraph, and then
select Format on the submenu, as shown:

Click here.

Drag down to here.

Then drag over
here and let go.

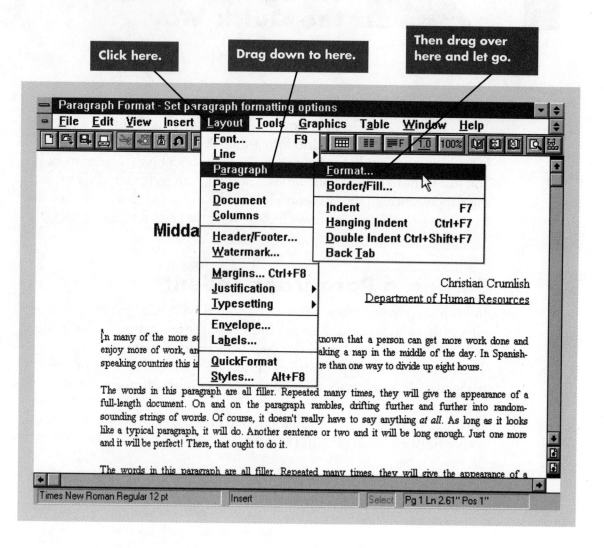

This brings up this dialog box:

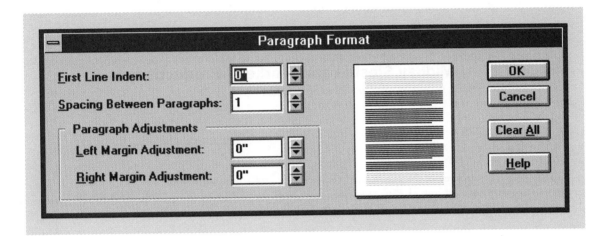

3. Type .5. (Don't type the second period; it's one of mine.)

4. Then click OK, as shown:

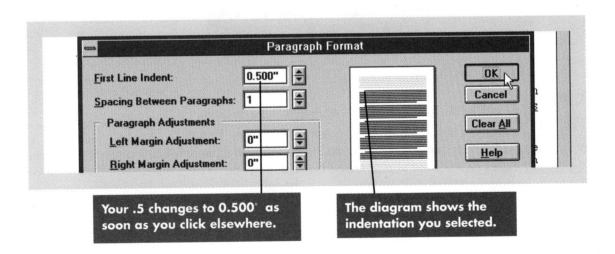

Your .5 changes to 0.500" as soon as you click elsewhere.

The diagram shows the indentation you selected.

All the paragraphs from the insertion point onward are now indented half an inch.

Midday Siestas and Workers' Productivity
A Proposal

Christian Crumlish
Department of Human Resources

In many of the more southerly countries it is well known that a person can get more work done and enjoy more of work, and indeed of life, simply by taking a nap in the middle of the day. In Spanish-speaking countries this is known as a *siesta*. There's more than one way to divide up eight hours.

The words in this paragraph are all filler. Repeated many times, they will give the appearance of a full-length document. On and on the paragraph rambles, drifting further and further into random-sounding strings of words. Of course, it doesn't really have to say anything *at all*. As long as it looks like a typical paragraph, it will do. Another sentence or two and it will be long enough. Just one more and it will be perfect! There, that ought to do it.

All the paragraphs are indented.

That's all you need to know.

• Note As with all the formatting we've discussed, you can set a paragraph indent just *before* you type a paragraph. Then all the following paragraphs you type will be indented as well. But there's no real need to plan ahead like that.

13

5 MINUTES

Double Spacing— the Editor's Friend

Most long documents will go through a few drafts before you're done with them. Even in this computer age, most people like to print things out on paper to read them over and see how they look on the page. If others are going to look at something you've written and offer suggestions or advice, they'll appreciate it if your document is double-spaced. For that matter, you'll like it too if you plan to reread your work and scribble changes or comments to yourself. You may even want your final documents double-spaced at times. I double-space these lessons when I submit them to my editor. (She makes me!)

When Single Spacing Just Isn't Enough

By now you know the drill. Changing line spacing is the kind of thing you want to do to all your paragraphs at once. As with all the formatting we've discussed, you *can* choose double spacing before you type your paragraphs, but then fewer lines will fit on the screen and you won't be able to see as much of your work as you go. So my advice is to wait till you're done typing. Of course, that's always my advice.

Like most useful formatting features, line spacing has a button on the
Power Bar:

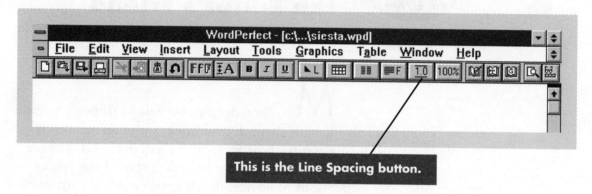

This is the Line Spacing button.

From your SIESTA report, follow these steps:

1. Place the insertion point at the beginning of the first paragraph (if it's not there already).

2. Click the Line Spacing button (and hold down the mouse
button). A menu drops down.

3. Select 2.0, as shown:

The paragraphs are now double-spaced.

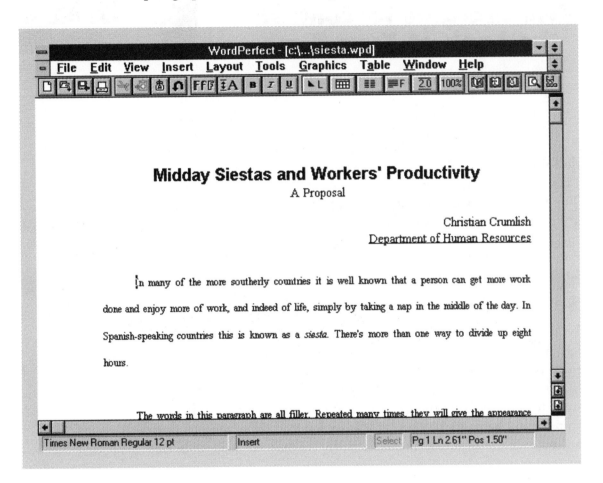

If or when you need to change your spacing back, go through the same steps—place the insertion point, click the Line Spacing button, and select 1.0.

5 MINUTES

Use Margins to Control the Look of Your Page

14

In the last few lessons, you've learned how to do formatting that affects paragraphs. In this lesson and the next few, I'll show you some things you can do to affect the look of the page. The margins (top and bottom, left and right) control where the words appear on the page. I'll show you how to change them and why you might want to.

Setting All the Margins at Once

WordPerfect starts you off with one-inch margins at the top, bottom, left, and right. You may find these margins, which are fairly standard, to be perfectly acceptable. But you may also want to change them. You may want to make your document seem longer, or shorter. You may want to make it easier to read. The Times Roman font can be sort of spindly and hard on the eyes, so let's set left and right margins to make a shorter line length, and increase the top margin to make a shorter page of text.

1. If you don't currently have SIESTA on the screen, switch to it or open it.

2. Pull down the Layout menu and select Margins, as shown:

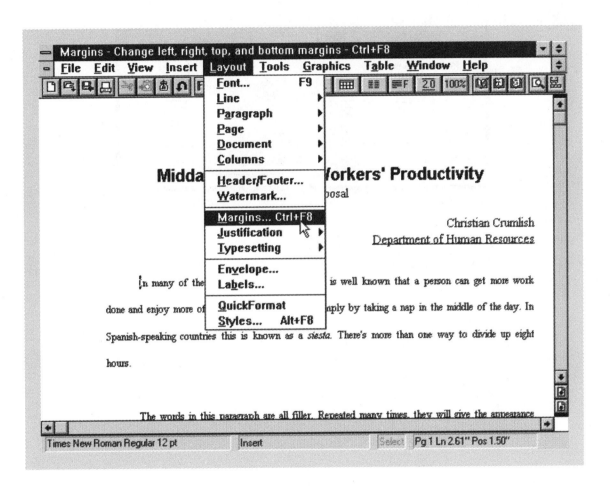

This dialog box will appear:

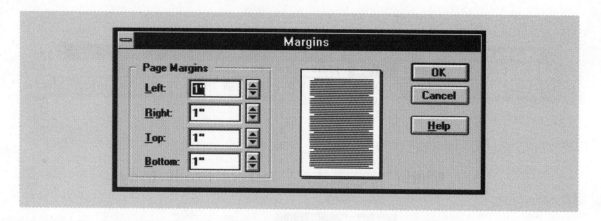

3. Type 1.25 and don't press ↵. (Hitting ↵ is like clicking OK, and you're not done yet.)

4. Press Tab.

5. Type 1.25 and press Tab again.

6. Type 1.25.

7. Now click OK, as shown:

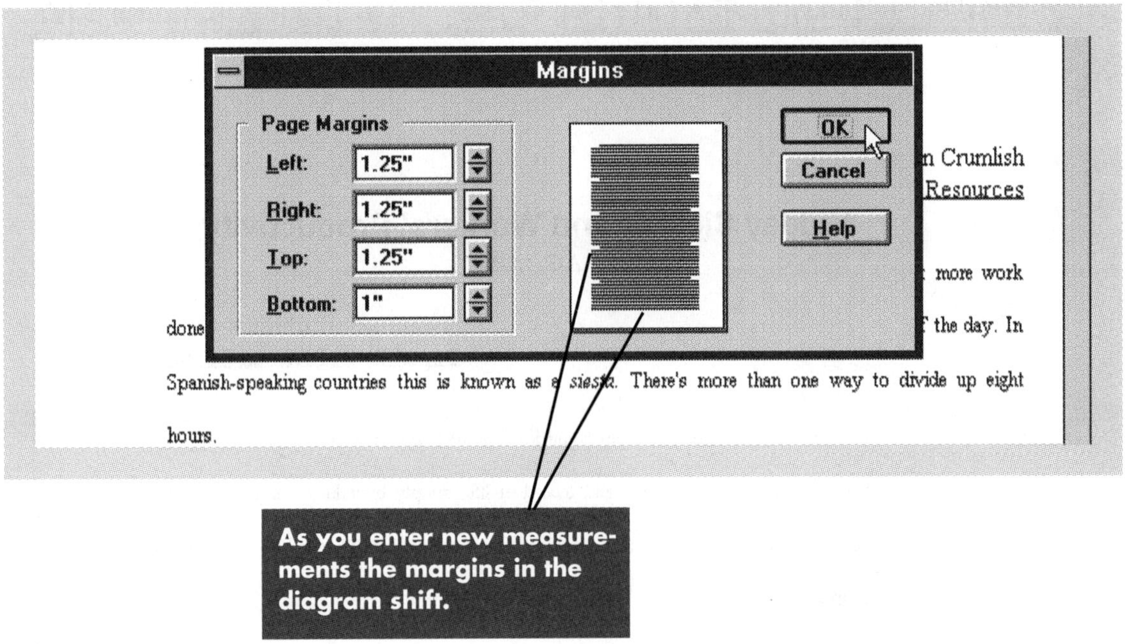

Margins
Page Margins
Left: 1.25"
Right: 1.25"
Top: 1.25"
Bottom: 1"

OK
Cancel
Help

...m Crumlish
...Resources

...more work

done... ...f the day. In

Spanish-speaking countries this is known as *el siesta*. There's more than one way to divide up eight

hours.

As you enter new measurements the margins in the diagram shift.

And here are your new margins (at least the top and left one):

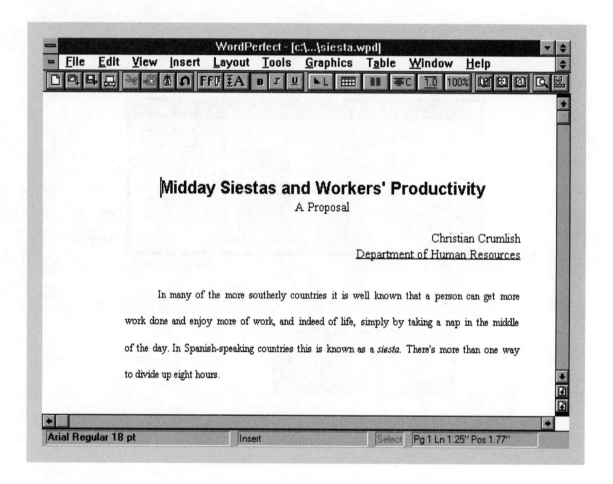

Now that you can see the margins in place on the page, you might want to change them again. You can change the left and right margins without going through the menus.

Changing Left and Right Margins with the Ruler Bar

The line length *does* look a little short now. Remember, we made the left margin an inch and a quarter. Here's how to drag it back to one inch with something called the *Ruler Bar*.

1. Pull down the <u>V</u>iew menu and select <u>R</u>uler Bar, as shown:

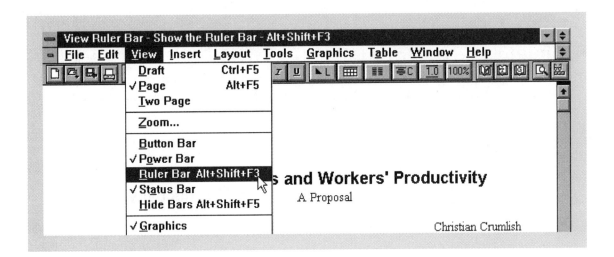

The Ruler Bar appears below the Power Bar. It includes margin and indent markers above a ruler, showing inches and tab settings:

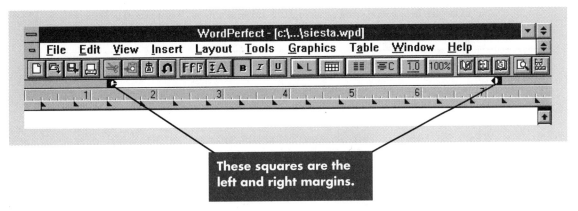

These squares are the left and right margins.

2. Click the left margin marker, and hold down the mouse button. A dotted line appears down the page.

3. Drag the marker to the one-inch mark on the ruler, as shown:

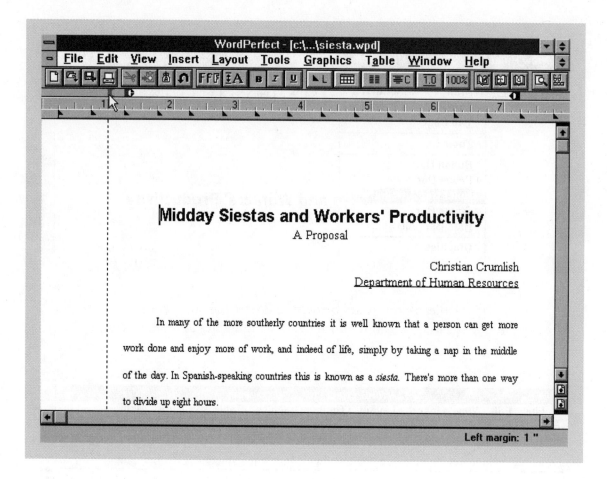

4. When the margin is in place, release the mouse button. The text reformats to the new left margin.

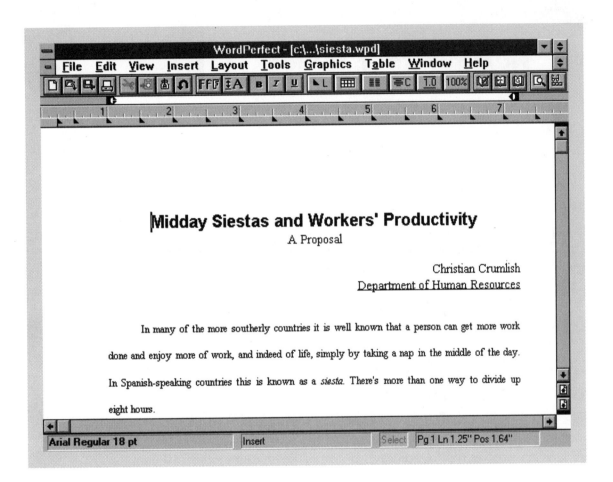

5. Pull down the View menu and select Ruler Bar again to make the Ruler Bar disappear.

In the next lesson I'll show you how to set up a header or footer to appear on every page.

Number Your Pages in a Flash

15

Now that I've got you thinking about how your pages will look, I'll move on to some other ways you can enhance the appearance of your documents. For instance, SIESTA is five pages long, right? How did you know that? Well, WordPerfect tells you—it shows up on the bottom of the screen. But what about your readers? They'd appreciate seeing page numbers. In this lesson I'll show you a very easy, straightforward way to set up automatic page numbers.

Insert Page Numbers with No Muss, No Fuss

The best thing about doing your page numbering with WordPerfect is that you only have do it once. You set up the numbers and then Word-Perfect makes sure they're accurate. If you make changes to your document and it gets longer or shorter, WordPerfect renumbers the pages. Here's what you do:

1. Pull down the Layout menu, select Page, and then select Numbering, as shown:

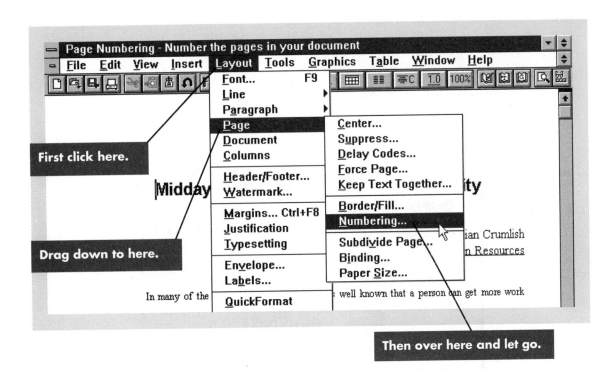

First click here.

Drag down to here.

Then over here and let go.

This dialog box appears:

Click here to select a position for your page numbers.

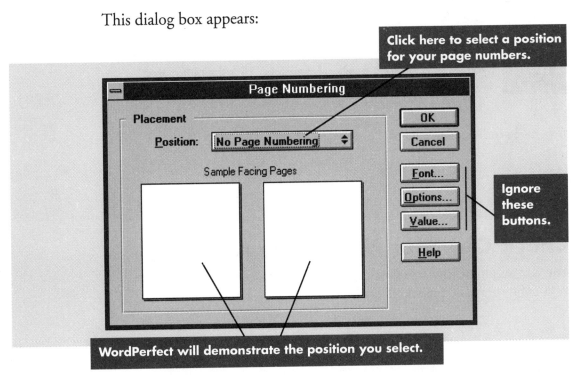

Ignore these buttons.

WordPerfect will demonstrate the position you select.

2. Click the button that reads **No Page Numbering** and hold
down the mouse button.

3. Drag the highlight down the menu that pops up and select
Bottom Center, as shown:

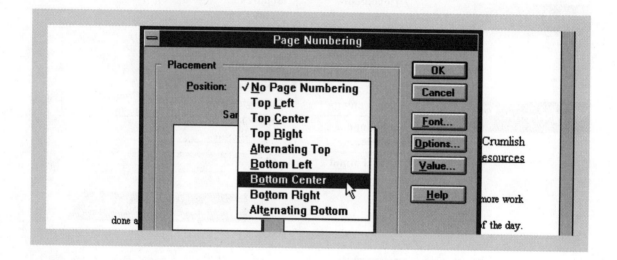

● Note If you select a different position by mistake, click the button and
choose again.

4. Click OK.

That's all there is to it.

Check Out Your New Page Numbers

You can scroll around to see your page numbers or you can look at a
two-page spread to get the overall feel. Here's how:

1. Pull down the <u>V</u>iew menu and select <u>T</u>wo Page, as shown:

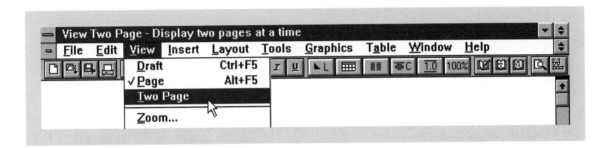

Pages 1 and 2 share the screen:

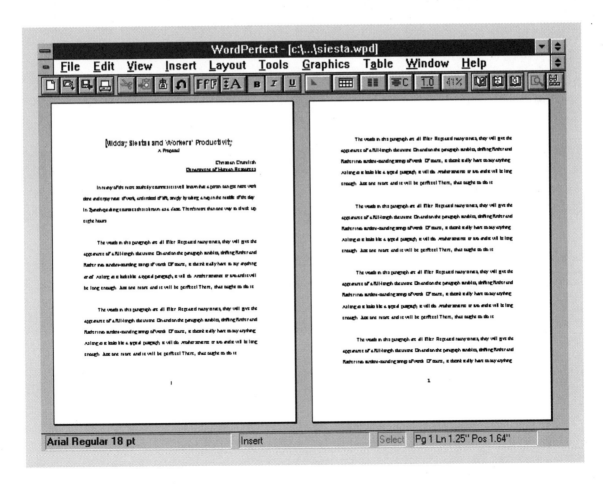

● Note Be careful. You can still edit your document in two-page view
and that means you can also mess it up accidentally.

When you've seen enough, switch back to the normal Page view:

2. Pull down the <u>V</u>iew menu and select <u>P</u>age, as shown:

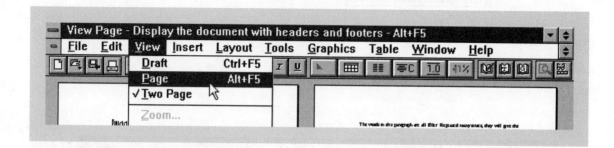

In the next lesson, I'll show you how to set up a header or footer to appear on every page.

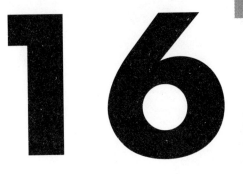

Straightforward Headers and Footers

Als long you want only a page number showing up on each page, you'll be fine using what you learned in the previous lesson. If you want something different—your name or a title on every page, the date of the current draft—you've got to set up a header or a footer. (A header is something that appears at the top—the *head*—of every page. A footer appears at the bottom—the *foot*.) But don't worry. It's still pretty easy.

Do You Want a Header or a Footer?

Okay, you don't have to decide just yet. Whether you want a header or a footer, it starts the same:

1. Pull down the Layout menu and select Header/Footer, as shown:

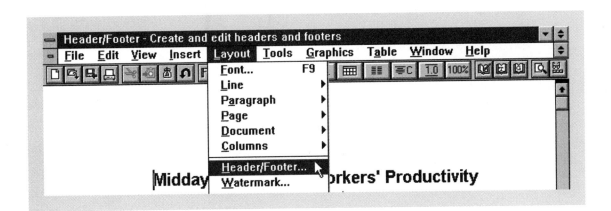

You'll see this dialog box:

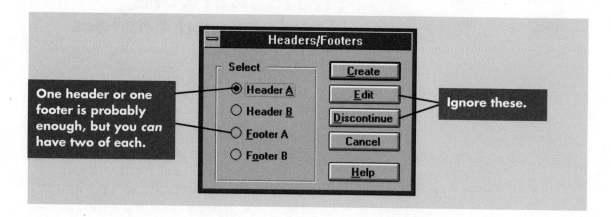

One header or one footer is probably enough, but you *can* have two of each.

Ignore these.

2. Click Footer A.

3. Click Create, as shown:

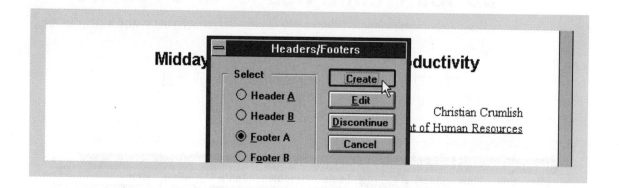

You are taken to the foot of the page, where your page number is, and a special Feature Bar™ appears. Ignore it.

This page number is here because you set it up in Lesson 15.

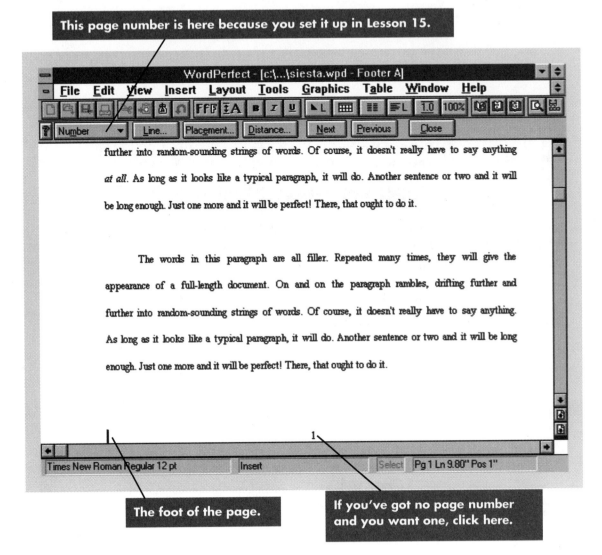

further into random-sounding strings of words. Of course, it doesn't really have to say anything *at all*. As long as it looks like a typical paragraph, it will do. Another sentence or two and it will be long enough. Just one more and it will be perfect! There, that ought to do it.

The words in this paragraph are all filler. Repeated many times, they will give the appearance of a full-length document. On and on the paragraph rambles, drifting further and further into random-sounding strings of words. Of course, it doesn't really have to say anything. As long as it looks like a typical paragraph, it will do. Another sentence or two and it will be long enough. Just one more and it will be perfect! There, that ought to do it.

The foot of the page.

If you've got no page number and you want one, click here.

4. Type the name you're using for the author of this report and then press Tab.

● Note Don't worry if the page number disappears. It's really still there.

Now, to insert today's date:

5. Pull down the Insert menu and select Date Text, as shown:

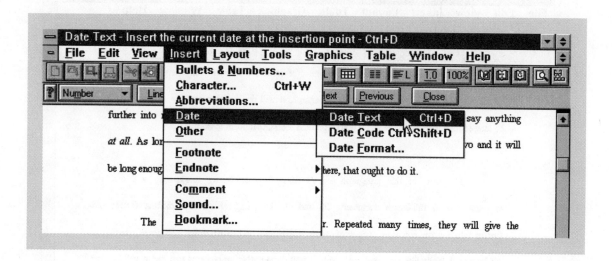

WordPerfect inserts today's date:

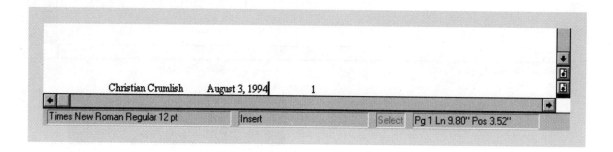

6. Click the Close button on the Feature Bar to make it go away, as shown:

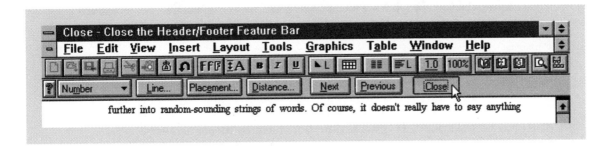

And that's all there is to setting up a footer. The steps are exactly the same for a header (except you have to select Header A in the Headers/Footers dialog box, of course).

If you want to change a header or footer later, the steps are almost the same. You just pull down Layout, select Header/Footer, click Header A or Footer A, and then click Edit instead of Create.

5 MINUTES

Make a Title Page

17

If you are writing a formal document, you may want it to have a title page. To give it one, you have to insert a special page break after the title information so that the actual text of the document starts on the second page. You also have to make any header or footer skip the first page. I'll show you how.

Force WordPerfect to Start a New Page

Normally, you don't have to tell WordPerfect when to start a new page. You just keep typing and when one page is full, a new one starts. In some ways this is similar to word wrap. You type a paragraph and Word-Perfect breaks the lines where they fit. At any point you can press ↵ and force WordPerfect to start a new line. So it shouldn't be too hard to remember that pressing Ctrl+↵ starts a new page. Try it now with SIESTA.

1. Position the insertion point just before the word *In* at the beginning of the first paragraph.

2. Press Ctrl+↵. The text after the insertion point is moved to the top of the second page.

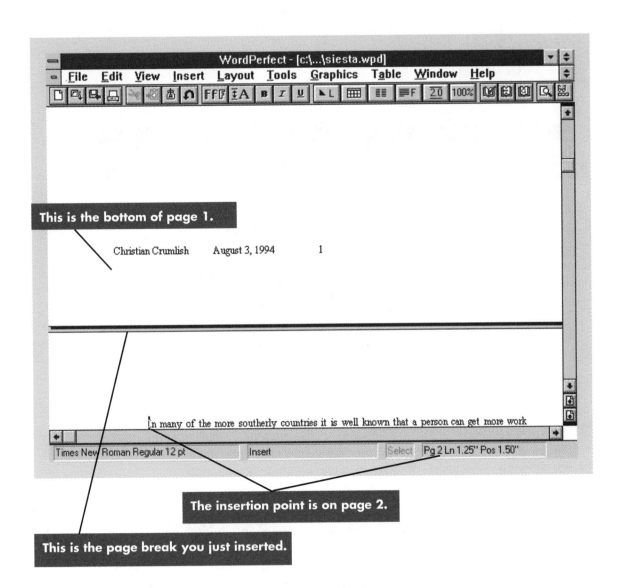

This is the bottom of page 1.

Christian Crumlish   August 3, 1994   1

In many of the more southerly countries it is well known that a person can get more work

The insertion point is on page 2.

This is the page break you just inserted.

Now the title info is on a page by itself. Of course, it's smack at the top of the page, so let's bring it down closer to the middle.

3. Press Ctrl+Home.

4. Pull down the Layout menu, select Page, and then select Center, as shown:

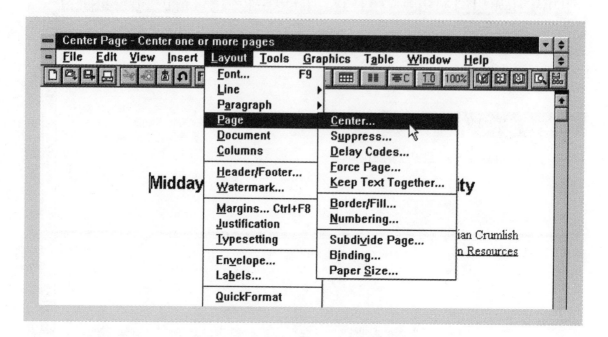

5. Select Current Page in the dialog box that appears:

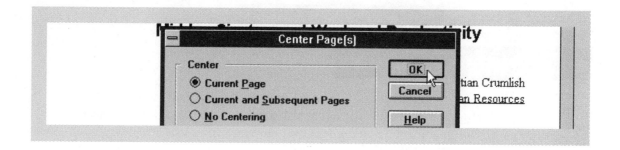

6. Click OK.

Now, let's looks at the first two pages at once:

7. Pull down the <u>V</u>iew menu and select <u>T</u>wo Page. You'll see the title page and page 2.

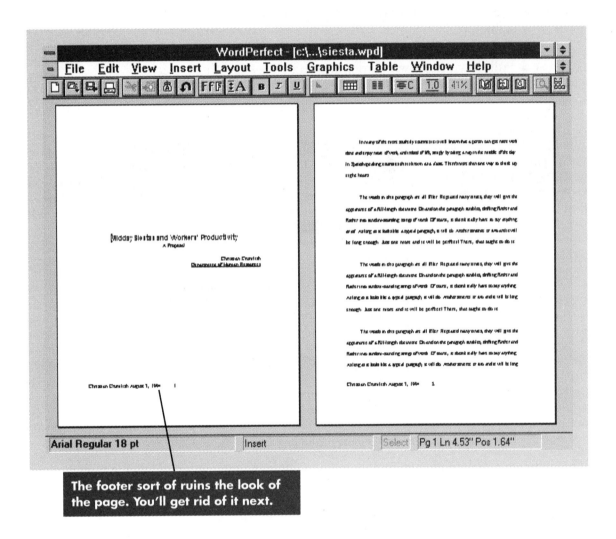

The footer sort of ruins the look of the page. You'll get rid of it next.

8. Pull down the <u>V</u>iew menu and select <u>P</u>age to switch back.

Quick & Easy

Remove Headers, Footers, and Page Numbers from Your Title Page

If you want to leave the footer off the title page, you have to tell Word-Perfect to *suppress* it.

1. Pull down the Layout menu, select Page, and then select Suppress, as shown:

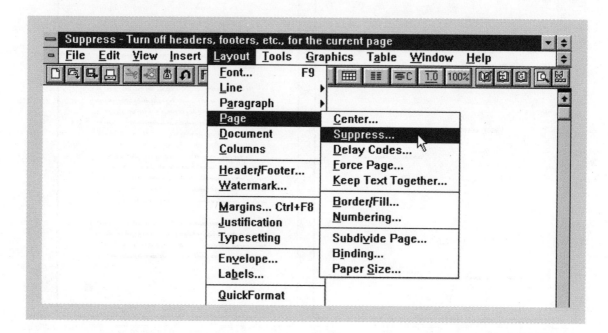

The following dialog box appears.

Suppress

Suppress on Current Page

☐ Header A	☐ Watermark A	**OK**
☐ Header B	☐ Watermark B	**Cancel**
☐ Footer A	☐ Page Numbering	**Help**
☐ Footer B	☐ All	

☐ Print Page Number at Bottom Center on Current Page

Check off Footer A *and* Page Numbering before you click OK.

Now view the title page as a whole.

2. Check off Footer A.

3. Check off Page Numbering.

4. Click OK, as shown:

Suppress

Suppress on Current Page

☐ Header A	☐ Watermark A	**OK**
☐ Header B	☐ Watermark B	**Cancel**
☒ Footer A	☒ Page Numbering	**Help**
☐ Footer B	☐ All	

That's it—A report ready for its audience. In the next and final part of this book, I'll show you how to revise and improve your documents.

PART THREE

Revise Your Work

Although computers allow you to make instant changes and to edit easily as you go, it's still better to write a whole draft without the distraction of editing. Don't let the finished look of text on the screen sucker you into trying to perfect it or second-guessing yourself as you write. It's better to make editing a separate task. Come back later, print your document out, look it over, and *then* make your changes.

In this part I'll show you more than simple retyping. You'll also see how to undo mistakes, copy and move text, make wholesale changes, check your spelling, and make shortcuts for your most common editing tasks.

Make Simple Changes and Corrections

18

Most of the editing you do to a document will be simple corrections. You print out the document, read it over, and mark your typos and the minor changes you want to make. Then you return to WordPerfect and touch up your document here and there. In this lesson I'll show you the basic set of editing techniques that you'll find yourself using most of the time.

Type New Text Over Old

Usually, if you position the insertion point and begin typing, the words to the right of the insertion point are pushed along ahead of the words you are typing. This is called *inserting text*. It is possible to switch from Insert mode to what WordPerfect calls *Typeover* mode (and some programs call Overtype). Then, when you position the insertion point and start typing, the letters you type replace the letters already there ("typing over" them). As you might imagine, this can be dangerous, but it's useful when you want to make a simple change. Let me show you an example. Start at the top of your SIESTA report.

Here's a new shortcut for jumping to the top of the next page:

1. Press Alt+PageDown. The top of page 2 appears on the screen.

2. Put the insertion point just before the letter *t* in the word *this*, on the third line of the first paragraph, as shown:

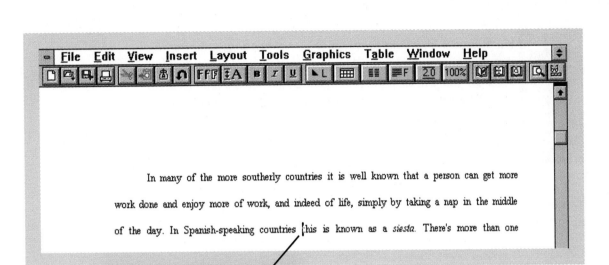

Put the insertion point here.

3. Press Insert (to the right of Backspace on most keyboards). This turns on Typeover.

4. Type **people call this** and watch as the new words replace the old.

5. Press Insert again. This turns Insert mode back on.

This last step is very important. You can easily wreak havoc with your document if you forget you are in Typeover mode.

> **● Note** Use Typeover only if the new text you intend to type is shorter than or the same length as old text you are replacing. (In the example you just tried, the new text was the same length as the old.) If the new text is longer, you'll replace text you don't want to unless you press **Insert** as soon as you reach the end of the text you intend to replace. Then it's probably not worth the bother of switching out of Insert mode.

There is also a way of indicating first what text you want to change, and then replacing it. We'll try that next.

Select the Text You Mean to Replace

Another basic editing move is to select the text you want to replace and then simply type the new text. As soon as you start typing, the selection disappears, essentially replaced by what you type. (This works in Insert mode, *not* in Typeover.)

> **● Note** If you want to keep the text you are replacing and use it elsewhere in your document, then you need to move it. We'll discuss moving text in Lesson 21.

Try it now.

1. Select **people call this**.

> In many of the more southerly countries it is well known that a person can get more work done and enjoy more of work, and indeed of life, simply by taking a nap in the middle of the day. In Spanish-speaking countries people call this a *siesta*. There's more than one way to divide up eight hours.

2. Type **such a nap is called** and watch as the selection disappears and the new text is inserted.

> In many of the more southerly countries it is well known that a person can get more work done and enjoy more of work, and indeed of life, simply by taking a nap in the middle of the day. In Spanish-speaking countries such a nap is called| a *siesta*. There's more than one way to divide up eight hours.

Easy, isn't it? This method also has its dangers. If you forget you have text selected and just start typing, you'll replace your selection by mistake. This is another good reason for saving your document from time to time. (In the next lesson, I'll show you how to undo *some* mistakes.)

Other times you will want to delete a large amount of text.

Delete Entire Selections

You can delete as much as you want, one letter at a time, with **Backspace** or **Delete**, as discussed in Lesson 2. But if you have a lot to get rid of, those methods are tedious. Once again, selecting the text first is the trick. Here's an example.

1. Press **PageDown**.

2. Press ↓ three times.

3. Select several sentences, beginning with *Of course* and ending with *perfect!* (and the space immediately after it), as shown.

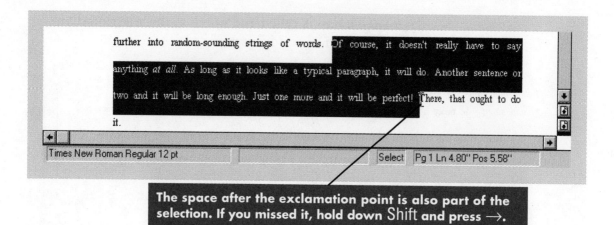

The space after the exclamation point is also part of the selection. If you missed it, hold down Shift and press →.

● **Note**   When you are deleting text, you have to pay attention to things like spaces and blank lines or they'll pile up on you.

3. Press Delete. The sentences disappear and the paragraph closes up.

> The words in this paragraph are all filler. Repeated many times, they will give the appearance of a full-length document. On and on the paragraph rambles, drifting further and further into random-sounding strings of words. There, that ought to do it.

There's one more shortcut I'd like to show you.

Delete a Word at a Time

You can also delete one word at a time. This is faster than going one letter at a time, but not so sweeping as deleting an entire selection all at once.

1. Press **Ctrl+Delete**. The word *There* disappears.

> The words in this paragraph are all filler. Repeated many times, they will give the appearance of a full-length document. On and on the paragraph rambles, drifting further and further into random-sounding strings of words. that ought to do it.

The word *There* is now gone, along with the comma that came after it.

Now delete the rest of the sentence a word at a time.

2. Press **Ctrl+Delete** five times.

> The words in this paragraph are all filler. Repeated many times, they will give the appearance of a full-length document. On and on the paragraph rambles, drifting further and further into random-sounding strings of words.

So **Ctrl+Delete** erases the word the insertion point is touching. (Remember, **Delete** by itself erases the letter to the right of the insertion point.)

This handful of tricks should be enough for most editing. In the next lesson, I'll show you how to undo a mistake.

19

I Wish I'da Never...

Oops! It's bound to happen eventually (if it hasn't already). By mistake, you delete the paragraph you just spent half an hour working on. What do you do? Fortunately, WordPerfect provides you with a way of recovering from most mistakes like this.

You can't take back something you just said, and you can't unring a bell, but you can undo many actions you take in WordPerfect. Now you can only undo the *most recent* action, so you have to think fast after you make a mistake. If you just keep pounding away at the keyboard, your error will be set in stone. Well, not entirely. This is another reason to save your work regularly. If you find yourself stuck with a really ugly mistake that you can't undo, you can go back to the last saved version of your document. In most cases, however, Undo will do the job.

The Do's and Don'ts of Undoing Your Mistakes

Actions you can undo include typing, deleting (probably the most important), and most menu commands. Let me show you a typical example. Start from your SIESTA report.

1. Press **Ctrl+End** to get to the end of the document.

2. Select the final paragraph, as shown.

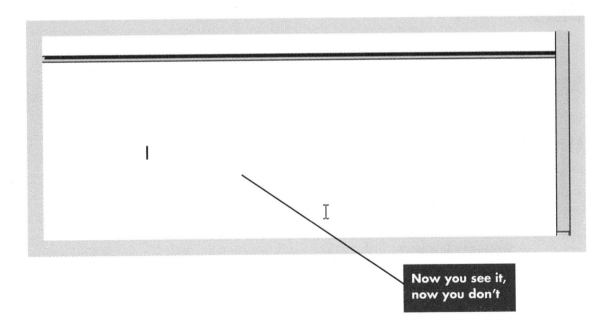

The words in this paragraph are all filler. Repeated many times, they will give the appearance of a full-length document. On and on the paragraph rambles, drifting further and further into random-sounding strings of words. Of course, it doesn't really have to say anything. As long as it looks like a typical paragraph, it will do. Another sentence or two and it will be long enough. Just one more and it will be perfect! There, that ought to do it.

3. Now, "accidentally" press **Delete**. The paragraph disappears. Oh no!

Now you see it, now you don't

But wait! All is not lost.

4. Click the Undo button on the Power Bar (the one with an arrow making a U-turn), as shown:

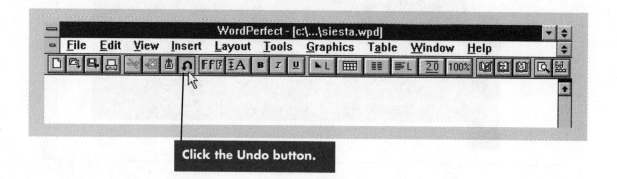

Click the Undo button.

The text reappears, intact.

● **Note** The Undo button is a slight shortcut for the Undo command on the Edit menu.

There are things that you can't undo. For example, you can't undo a save.

Undo that Undo that You Do So Well

One of the things that you can undo is the Undo command itself. Why would you want to do this? Well, say you changed your mind, or realized that you actually *had* done what you intended. Here's an example:

1. Select the last paragraph again now.

2. Press **Delete**, accidentally on purpose.

3. Pull down the Edit menu and select Undo (or click the Undo button—same effect either way).

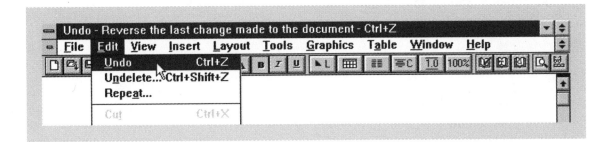

The paragraph reappears.

4. Now, pull down the Edit menu again, and select Undo again.

Now the paragraph is gone again. You can change your mind in this manner indefinitely.

5. Pull down the Edit menu and select Undo a third time.

Now it's back again.

If Worse Comes to Worse

If you screwed something up so badly that you'd give up your last half hour's work (or however much work you've done since you last saved) to fix it, there's something you can do even if you can't undo. It goes like this:

1. Pull down the File menu and select Exit.

2. When asked if you want to save changes to the document in which you made the mistake, click No.

3. Save the changes to other documents you had open, if any.

4. Run WordPerfect again.

5. Open the document (it will be at the bottom of the File menu).

Do this only if the mistake is so bad that you can afford to lose whatever other work you may have done since the last time you saved.

That's about all you need to know. In the upcoming lessons I'll be showing you other ways of editing your documents.

20

Easy Editing with Drag and Drop

In this lesson I'll show you a new WordPerfect feature that really makes editing easier. It's called *drag and drop* and it allows you to click on a selection and drag it to a new location.

This is the way all word processors should work, because it allows you to grab letters, words, or even whole sentences or paragraphs, and move them (or copy them) directly to a new location in your document. If you notice that you've accidentally switched two characters, you can drag one into the correct place. You can move a phrase from the beginning of the sentence to another part of the sentence. The possibilities are endless. I'll show you first how to move text and then how to copy.

Move Text with Drag and Drop

Rearranging text is a common job in editing a document. Drag and drop is such an easy way to do it that it hardly needs an introduction. Try it now with the SIESTA report. Start at the top of the document.

1. Press Alt+PageDown.

2. Press PageDown.

3. Press ↓ eight times.

Your screen should look like this:

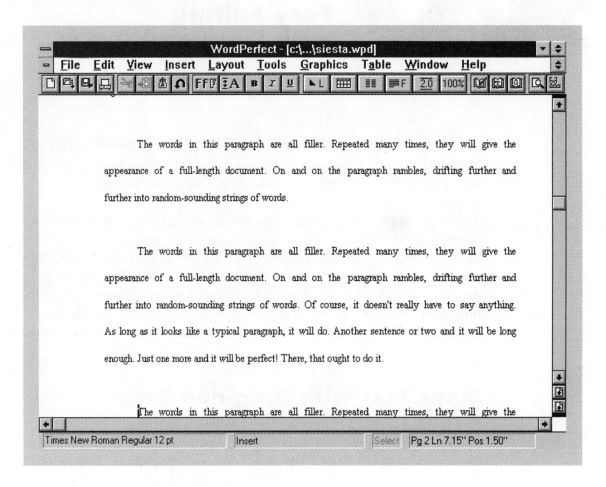

4. Select the second sentence in the first paragraph.

> The words in this paragraph are all filler. Repeated many times, they will give the appearance of a full-length document. On and on the paragraph rambles, drifting further and further into random-sounding strings of words.

Make sure you include the space that comes at the end. (This will happen automatically if you select the sentence by triple-clicking.)

5. If it's not there already, move the mouse pointer to the selection. It will change from an insertion point to an arrow.

6. Click (and hold down) the mouse button. A gray box with a dotted shadow appears at the stem of the mouse pointer.

> The words in this paragraph are all filler. Repeated many times, they will give the appearance of a full-length document. On and on the paragraph rambles, drifting further and further into random-sounding strings of words.

● Note You may find occasionally that you have started dragging a selection by mistake. This might happen when you try to redo a selection that's not quite right. If you accidentally start inside the first selection, you'll be dragging it. Just release the mouse button, and then click the Undo button, if necessary.

7. While still holding down the mouse button, drag the pointer until the insertion point that moves with it is to the left of the *R* at the beginning of the second sentence

in the next paragraph, as shown:

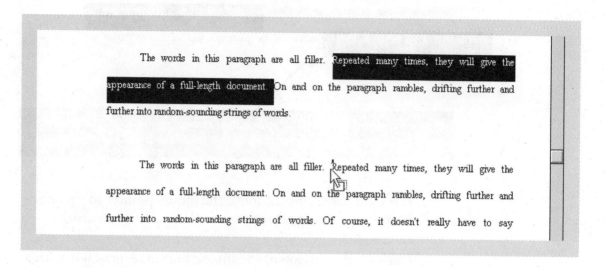

If you accidentally let go of the mouse button and lose your selection, just go back to step 4 and start over.

8. With the pointer in place, release the mouse button. The selection appears in the new location.

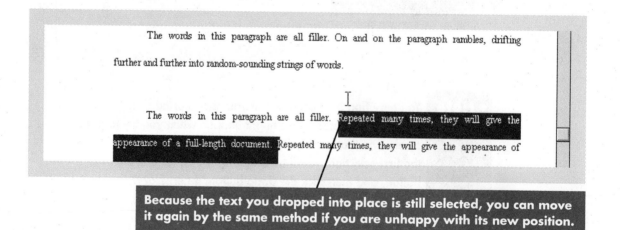

Because the text you dropped into place is still selected, you can move it again by the same method if you are unhappy with its new position.

It's that easy.

> **● Note**   One drawback of drag and drop is that if you drag a selection
> past the bottom or top of the screen, the view scrolls very
> rapidly, making it difficult to drop the selection in a specific
> location more than one screen away from where you started. If
> this poses a problem for you, try the cut-and-paste approach
> described in the next lesson.

Copy Text with Drag and Drop

You copy text almost exactly the same way as you move it with drag
and drop. The difference is that you hold down Ctrl first. Try it.

1. Select *and on* (and the space after *on*) in the second paragraph, as shown:

The words in this paragraph are all filler. Repeated many times, they will give the

appearance of a full-length document. Repeated many times, they will give the appearance of

a full-length document. On and on the paragraph rambles, drifting further and further into

random-sounding strings of words. Of course, it doesn't really have to say anything. As long

> **If you don't get this space at the end of the selection,
> words will run together when you move it.**

2. Point to the selection with the arrow.

3. Hold down Ctrl and then click (and hold down) the mouse
button. A gray box with a solid shadow appears at the stem
of the mouse pointer.

4. Drag the arrow until the insertion point is just before the *t*
in the word *the* that comes immediately after the selection,
as shown:

> The words in this paragraph are all filler. Repeated many times, they will give the
> appearance of a full-length document. Repeated many times, they will give the appearance of
> a full-length document. On and on the paragraph rambles, drifting further and further into
> random-sounding strings of words. Of course, it doesn't really have to say anything. As long

5. Release the mouse button and Ctrl. The selection is copied
(and now the copy is selected).

> The words in this paragraph are all filler. Repeated many times, they will give the
> appearance of a full-length document. Repeated many times, they will give the appearance of
> a full-length document. On and on and on the paragraph rambles, drifting further and further
> into random-sounding strings of words. Of course, it doesn't really have to say anything. As

That's all there is to drag and drop.

LESSON 21

21 Rearrange Text with Cut, Copy, and Paste

5 MINUTES

In the previous lesson I mentioned one drawback to drag and drop: it is hard to control if you need to scroll to the destination. So when you need more control, there is another way to move and copy text.

To move text, you cut it and then paste it elsewhere. If you copy and then paste, the original text is not moved.

Cut-and-Paste Editing

When you cut selected text, it is removed from the document but saved on something called the *Clipboard*. Then when you paste it, it is copied from the Clipboard to the new location.

Try it now with the memo you wrote in Part One.

1. Open memo.wpd (or switch to it if you already have it open).

2. Select the first sentence in the second paragraph.

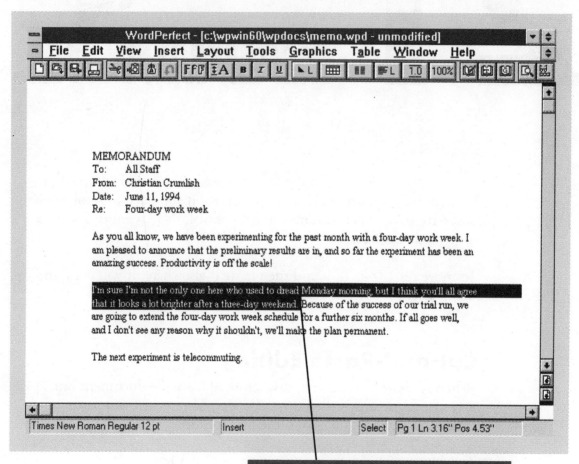

MEMORANDUM
To: All Staff
From: Christian Crumlish
Date: June 11, 1994
Re: Four-day work week

As you all know, we have been experimenting for the past month with a four-day work week. I am pleased to announce that the preliminary results are in, and so far the experiment has been an amazing success. Productivity is off the scale!

I'm sure I'm not the only one here who used to dread Monday morning, but I think you'll all agree that it looks a lot brighter after a three-day weekend. Because of the success of our trial run, we are going to extend the four-day work week schedule for a further six months. If all goes well, and I don't see any reason why it shouldn't, we'll make the plan permanent.

The next experiment is telecommuting.

Again, it is important that your selection include this space after the sentence.

3. Click the Cut button on the Power Bar (the one with a pair of scissors on it, to the right of the Print button), as shown:

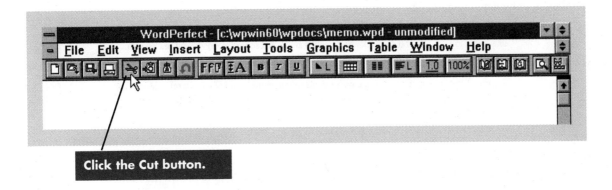

Click the Cut button.

● **Note** The Cut button is a slight shortcut for the Cut command on the Edit menu.

The text disappears:

As you all know, we have been experimenting for the past month with a four-day work week. I am pleased to announce that the preliminary results are in, and so far the experiment has been an amazing success. Productivity is off the scale!

Because of the success of our trial run, we are going to extend the four-day work week schedule for a further six months. If all goes well, and I don't see any reason why it shouldn't, we'll make the plan permanent.

Don't worry, though. It's on the Clipboard I mentioned earlier.

4. Move the insertion point just to the left of the *I* in the word *If* that begins the next sentence, as shown:

As you all know, we have been experimenting for the past month with a four-day work week. I am pleased to announce that the preliminary results are in, and so far the experiment has been an amazing success. Productivity is off the scale!

Because of the success of our trial run, we are going to extend the four-day work week schedule for a further six months. If all goes well, and I don't see any reason why it shouldn't, we'll make the plan permanent.

5. Click the Paste button on the Power Bar (to the left of the Undo button—the picture on it is supposed to be a paste pot), as shown:

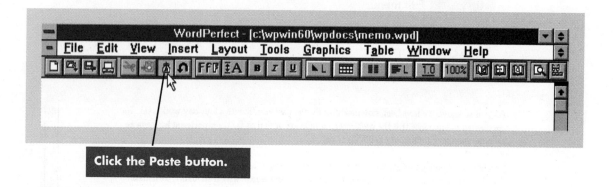

Click the Paste button.

• Note The Paste button is a slight shortcut for the Paste command on the Edit menu.

The sentence is pasted in the new location.

am pleased to announce that the preliminary results are in, and so far the experiment has been an amazing success. Productivity is off the scale!

Because of the success of our trial run, we are going to extend the four-day work week schedule for a further six months. I'm sure I'm not the only one here who used to dread Monday morning, but I think you'll all agree that it looks a lot brighter after a three-day weekend. If all goes well, and I don't see any reason why it shouldn't, we'll make the plan permanent.

The sentence is also still on the Clipboard. (It will stay on the Clipboard until something new is copied or cut, or until you quit Windows.)

6. Click the Paste button again. The sentence is pasted in a second time.

Because of the success of our trial run, we are going to extend the four-day work week schedule for a further six months. I'm sure I'm not the only one here who used to dread Monday morning, but I think you'll all agree that it looks a lot brighter after a three-day weekend. I'm sure I'm not the only one here who used to dread Monday morning, but I think you'll all agree that it looks a lot brighter after a three-day weekend. If all goes well, and I don't see any reason why it shouldn't, we'll make the plan permanent.

Here is the sentence once.

And here it is again.

You don't really want a second copy of that sentence, do you?

7. Click the Undo button.

Now I'll show you how to copy text (the steps are very similar).

Copying (and Pasting)

When you cut and paste, the text is removed from its original location. The only difference when you copy and paste is that the text remains in its original location.

1. Select the short sentence at the end of the first paragraph.

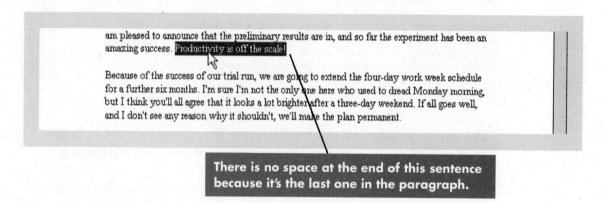

am pleased to announce that the preliminary results are in, and so far the experiment has been an amazing success. Productivity is off the scale!

Because of the success of our trial run, we are going to extend the four-day work week schedule for a further six months. I'm sure I'm not the only one here who used to dread Monday morning, but I think you'll all agree that it looks a lot brighter after a three-day weekend. If all goes well, and I don't see any reason why it shouldn't, we'll make the plan permanent.

There is no space at the end of this sentence because it's the last one in the paragraph.

2. Click the Copy button on the Power Bar (the one with a tiny clipboard and a teeny-tiny arrow going to it, to the right of the Cut button), as shown:

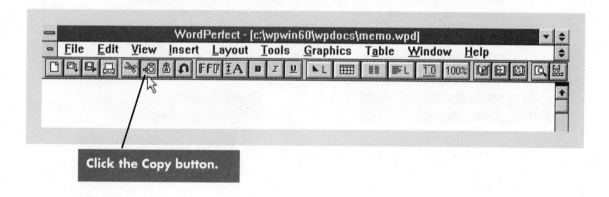

WordPerfect - [c:\wpwin60\wpdocs\memo.wpd]

File   Edit   View   Insert   Layout   Tools   Graphics   Table   Window   Help

Click the Copy button.

● Note The Copy button is a slight shortcut for the Copy command on the Edit menu.

3. Now move the insertion point to the beginning of the last sentence in the memo.

As you all know, we have been experimenting for the past month with a four-day work week. I am pleased to announce that the preliminary results are in, and so far the experiment has been an amazing success. Productivity is off the scale!

Because of the success of our trial run, we are going to extend the four-day work week schedule for a further six months. I'm sure I'm not the only one here who used to dread Monday morning, but I think you'll all agree that it looks a lot brighter after a three-day weekend. If all goes well, and I don't see any reason why it shouldn't, we'll make the plan permanent.

The next experiment is telecommuting.

4. Click the Paste button. The sentence is pasted in the new location.

As you all know, we have been experimenting for the past month with a four-day work week. I am pleased to announce that the preliminary results are in, and so far the experiment has been an amazing success. Productivity is off the scale!

Because of the success of our trial run, we are going to extend the four-day work week schedule for a further six months. I'm sure I'm not the only one here who used to dread Monday morning, but I think you'll all agree that it looks a lot brighter after a three-day weekend. If all goes well, and I don't see any reason why it shouldn't, we'll make the plan permanent.

Productivity is off the scale!The next experiment is telecommuting.

The sentences run together here because there was no space after the sentence you copied.

5. Type a space.

6. Press Home.

7. Press Delete.

8. Type I'll say it again, p (to provide an introductory phrase).

> Because of the success of our trial run, we are going to extend the four-day work week schedule for a further six months. I'm sure I'm not the only one here who used to dread Monday morning, but I think you'll all agree that it looks a lot brighter after a three-day weekend. If all goes well, and I don't see any reason why it shouldn't, we'll make the plan permanent.
>
> I'll say it again, productivity is off the scale! The next experiment is telecommuting.

As with cutting, the sentence is still on the Clipboard and could be pasted in anywhere repeatedly.

There is one other use for cut, copy, and paste worth knowing.

Copy from One Document to Another

You may sometimes be able to save yourself some work by copying a sentence or paragraph to a different document, even if you'll then need to edit it slightly. It's almost as easy to do this as it is to copy within a document.

1. In your memo, select from the word *we* all the way to the end of the first sentence of the first paragraph (as usual, include the space that comes after the sentence in your selection).

> From: Christian Crumlish
> Date: June 11, 1994
> Re: Four-day work week
>
> As you all know, we have been experimenting for the past month with a four-day work week. I am pleased to announce that the preliminary results are in, and so far the experiment has been an amazing success. Productivity is off the scale!

2. Click the Copy button.

3. Pull down the <u>W</u>indow menu and select **siesta.wpd** (or open it if it's no longer open).

4. Put the insertion point just before the first word of the first sentence of the second paragraph, as shown:

way to divide up eight hours.

The words in this paragraph are all filler. On and on the paragraph rambles, drifting further and further into random-sounding strings of words.

5. Click the Paste button. The text from the memo appears.

we have been experimenting for the past month with a four-day work week. The words in this paragraph are all filler. On and on the paragraph rambles, drifting further and further into random-sounding strings of words.

6. Press Home.

7. Press Delete.

8. Type W.

We have been experimenting for the past month with a four-day work week. The words in this paragraph are all filler. On and on the paragraph rambles, drifting further and further into random-sounding strings of words.

So that's how you copy from one document to another. You can do the same thing with cut and paste as well. Remember to save all the changes you've made to memo.wpd and siesta.wpd.

In the next lesson I'll show you how to search for specific words in your documents and how to change them automatically.

22

Find Words and Replace Them with Other Words

If you're looking for a specific word or phrase in your document (say, a sentence you wanted to reread and possibly change), WordPerfect can help you find it. If you want to substitute a better word for one somewhere in your document, WordPerfect can replace it for you.

In this lesson, I'll show you how to find words and how to replace the words you find. (Replacing is more fun.)

Seek and Ye Shall Find

If you don't have SIESTA open, open it. And if you're not at the top of the document, press Ctrl+Home to get there.

Finding a specific word in a document is easy. Take, for example, the word *experimenting*. In the previous lesson, you copied a phrase that included that word. What if you don't remember where you put it, exactly? No problem. Just go along with the following steps.

1. Pull down the Edit menu and select Find, as shown:

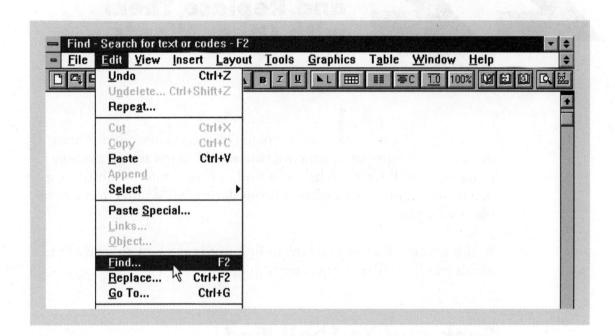

You'll see this dialog box:

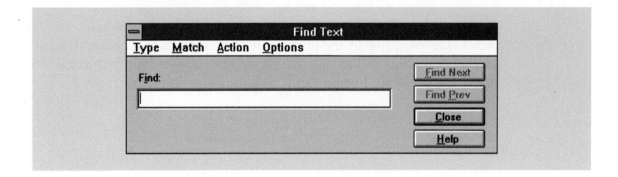

Was the word *experiment* or *experimenting*? If you don't remember, it's safe to search for the shorter word (since it's also part of the longer one).

2. Type experiment. (Don't type the period.)

● Note If you hit ↵ after typing your word, it has the same effect as clicking F̲ind Next. That may work out just fine, but you should develop the habit of *not* just hitting ↵ when typing in a dialog box because sometimes you'll have other things to do first before clicking OK or whatever. (In this case, though, there is nothing else to do first.)

3. Click F̲ind Next. WordPerfect finds *experiment* and highlights it.

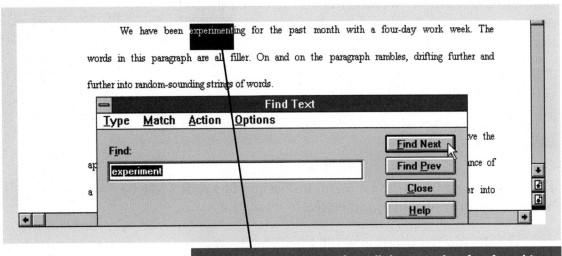

It was *experimenting* after all, but WordPerfect found it anyway. Notice that only part of the word is highlighted.

That's how you find words. When you're done finding things, you've got to get out of this dialog box.

4. Click C̲lose.

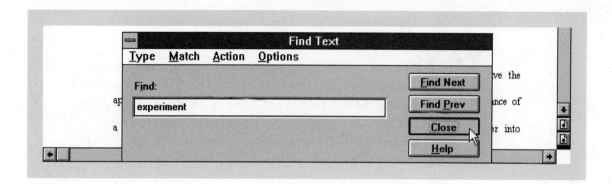

Replace One Word with Another

But wait. There's more. WordPerfect also gives you the ability to re-place one word with another. It can be a smooth way to edit. Don't like that word? Replace it!

● **Note** It's always a good idea to save your document before replacing words. That way if you screw things up royally, you can just close the document without saving it and then reopen it in its unscrewed-up form.

The next paragraph in SIESTA mentions "strings of words." Maybe "streams of words" would sound better.

1. If your last selection is still highlighted, press ←.

● **Note** You don't need to know why you just did that, but if you don't do it, it messes up the replacing. (Trust me on this.)

2. Pull down the Edit menu and select Replace, as shown:

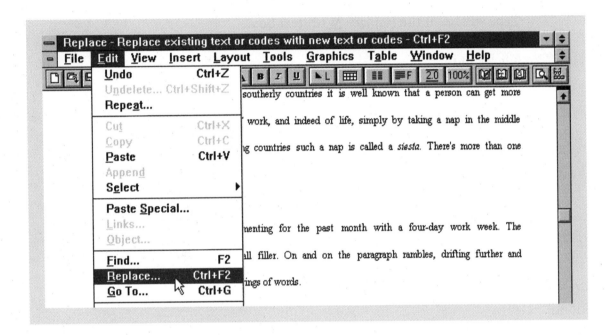

This dialog box appears.

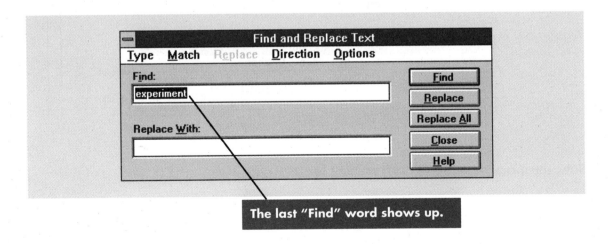

The last "Find" word shows up.

3. Type string in the Find text box (*don't* press ↵).

4. Press Tab.

5. Type stream in the Replace With text box.

6. Click Find.

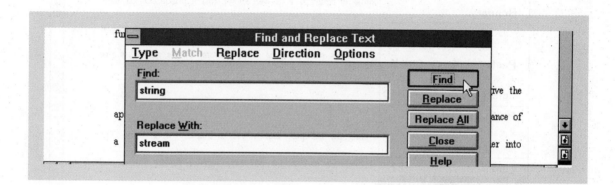

Found!

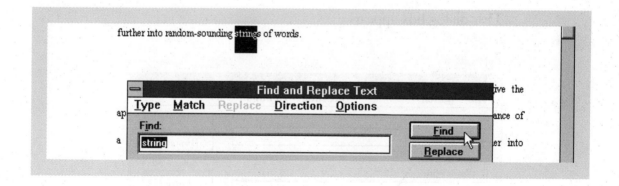

Now, the moment we've all been waiting for.

7. Click Replace.

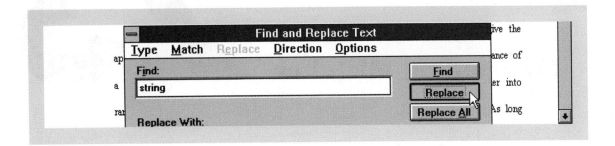

It's done. I know it appears as though nothing has happened. The word *string* is still highlighted. But you're actually looking at the *next* paragraph. (The scroll box is a little lower on the right.) You see, choosing the Replace button replaces the word, and moves you to the next occurrence of the word, if there is any (just as Find and Find next do). That's so you can make the same switch over and over. But let's make sure *stream* really did replace *string*.

8. Click Close.

Look at the paragraph above the selection. See, it did change.

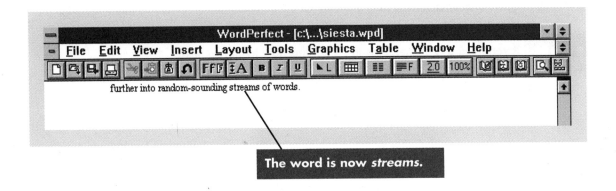

The word is now *streams*.

That's all you really need to know about Find and Replace.

Fix Spelling Mistakes

2 **3**

Wouldn't it be nice to have an assistant just to check all your spelling? WordPerfect provides you with the next best thing—a Speller, called, appropriately enough, Speller. The Speller compares your spellings to its internal dictionary. When you're trying to write, you shouldn't have to worry about spelling or typos. With Word-Perfect, you can write freely, then go back and check easily.

Grist for the Mill

First, to give the Speller a workout, you'll need to enter a sample paragraph.

1. Start a new document.

● Note If you need a refresher, Lesson 7 explains how to start a new document.

2. Type the following paragraph, warts and all:

Job-related stress can sometimes be aleviated by by doing a simple stretching excercise or by saying a nonsense word, such as "mang." It is good to stand up and leave your desk even if you do not plan to excercise, according to Dr. Grieble. The point is to interrupt your routine . ↵

> Job-related stress can sometimes be alleviated by by doing a simple stretching exercise or by saying a nonsense word, such as "mang." It is good to stand up and leave your desk even if you do not plan to excercise, according to Dr. Grieble. THe point is to interrupt your routine.

There is an abundance of errors in this poor paragraph. Let's see how many WordPerfect can catch.

No More I Before E

Okay, maybe you can't afford to forget all the spelling rules you ever learned, but you can count on WordPerfect to find glaring errors.

You can start the Speller from anywhere in your document. Then, when the Speller reaches the end, it will ask you whether it should continue from the start. But you might as well begin at the beginning.

• Note To check the spelling of a single word you are unsure of, select the word before starting the spelling check. After WordPerfect checks the spelling of that particular word, it will ask you if you want to continue checking the rest of the document.

1. Press Ctrl+Home.

Quick&Easy

2. Click the Speller button on the Toolbar (the one with an
open book and a checkmark), as shown:

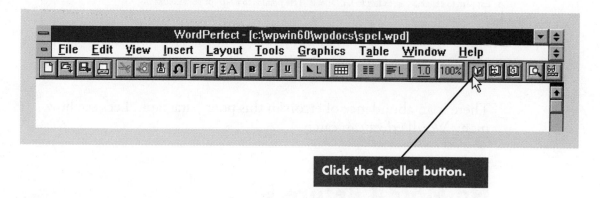

Click the Speller button.

This dialog box appears:

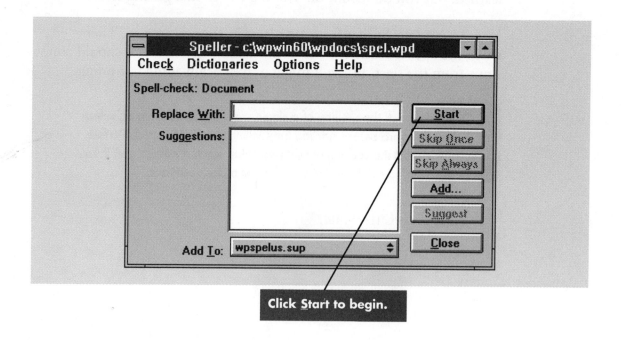

Click Start to begin.

● Note You can quit a spelling check at any time by clicking Close.

3. Click the <u>S</u>tart button to start the spell check. WordPerfect catches the first mistake.

The first mistake is *alleviated*, which has two *l*s. When the Speller's suggestion is correct, as it is now, you tell it to make the change.

4. Click the Replace button.

Job-related stress can sometimes be alleviated by by doing a simple stretching exercise or by saying a nonsense word, such as "mang." It is good to stand up and leave your desk even if you do not plan to excercise, according to Dr. Grieble. THe point is to interrupt your routine.

Speller - c:\wpwin60\wpdocs\spel.wpd

Check   Dictio<u>n</u>aries   <u>O</u>ptions   <u>H</u>elp

Not found: aleviated

Replace <u>W</u>ith: | alleviated | | **Replace** |

Sugg<u>e</u>stions: | alleviated | | **Skip <u>O</u>nce** |
| elevated | | **Skip <u>A</u>lways** |

WordPerfect's first suggestion is correct. When a different suggestion is the right one, click on it before making the change.

Another word is questioned. In this case, the problem is the double *by by*. The dialog box changes slightly for this situation.

5. Click <u>R</u>eplace.

Quick & Easy

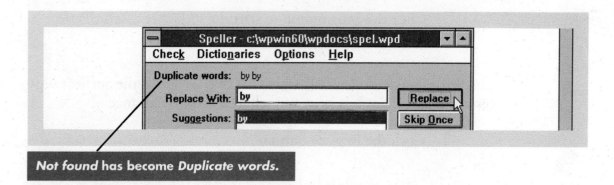

Not found has become **Duplicate words.**

The next incorrect word the Speller catches is *excercise*. Even though
this error appears in more than one place, you have to correct it only
once and WordPerfect will do the rest. (Imagine if you had misspelled a
word throughout a 50-page report and had to change each one!)

6. Click Replace.

Now the Speller can't find *mang* in the dictionary, which is reassuring.
Tell the Speller to skip this one.

7. Click Skip Once.

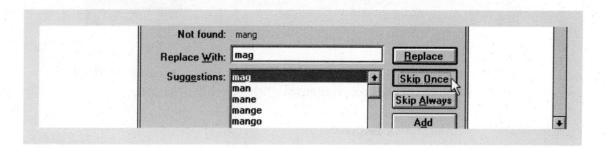

● Note Don't be concerned if you notice that the second *excercise* has
not been corrected yet. It will happen automatically when
WordPerfect gets to it.

Grieble, a proper name, could not be found in the dictionary. You'll probably use this name again if you used it once, so add it to the dictionary or you'll have to skip it over and over in the future.

8. Click Add.

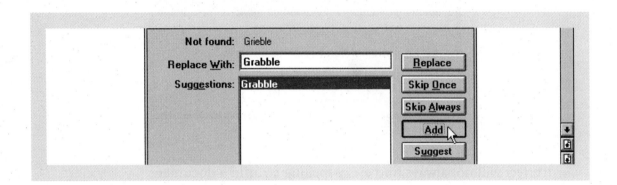

Another kind of typo is discovered—the kind where you didn't let up on Shift in time.

9. Press ↓ twice to highlight The.

10. Click Replace again.

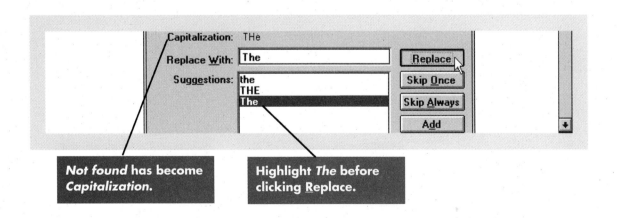

Not found has become **Capitalization.**

Highlight *The* **before clicking Replace.**

A dialog box appears to tell you that your spell check is finished.

11. Click <u>Y</u>es.

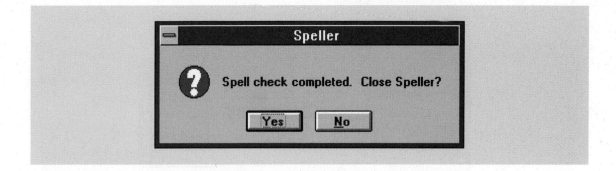

WordPerfect will not always find every spelling error in a document.
For instance, some misspelled words are just different words spelled cor-
rectly. WordPerfect will never catch that type of mistake, so don't rely
on it completely. Keep a dictionary handy.

24

Button Bar, Button Bar, Who's Got the Button Bar?

5 MINUTES

If you're happy using the menus and the Power Bar for your most common actions with WordPerfect, then you may not want to bother with this lesson. The commands on the Power Bar cover the vast majority of actions you'll ever want to take with Word-Perfect, and the menus are fairly easy to thumb through when you're stuck.

Still, WordPerfect supplies you with a set of Button Bars (in addition to the Power Bar) that you can also display on the screen and choose commands from.

If you're looking for more shortcuts for the things you're doing all the time, you might want to take a look at these Button Bars.

• Note You may remember that I asked you to hide this same Button Bar at the end of Lesson 1.

Bring Out Your Button Bars

First of all, here's how to display a Button Bar:

1. Open a new document. (See Lesson 7 if you need a refresher).

2. Click the View Button Bar button, the rightmost one on the Power Bar, as shown:

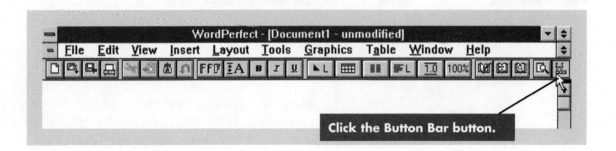

A Button Bar appears (it's called the WordPerfect Button Bar):

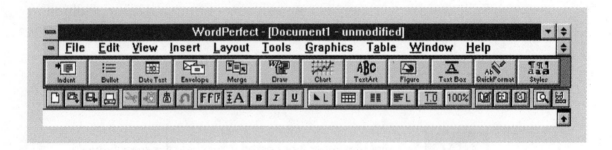

This is truly the second-string shortcut bar (as compared to the Power Bar). You may never need to use any of the buttons on it unless you'll be sending mass mailings (then the Merge button will come in handy), or creating charts for presentations (the Chart button).

Don't Like That One? Have Another

There *are* other Button Bars to choose from.

1. Put the mouse pointer in the dark gray background area of the Button Bar and click the *right* mouse button (and hold it down). A menu pops up.

2. Select Font on the menu, as shown:

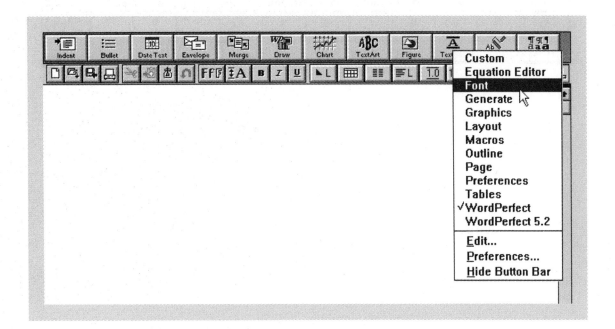

The Font Button Bar appears, full of nothing but Font (character appearance) shortcuts. If you're doing a lot of formatting, this one might come in handy.

You can also stick Button Bars in different parts of the screen, depending on what works best for you.

Put the Button Bar Where You Want It

Button Bars are easy to move and position on the screen.

1. Put the mouse pointer in the dark gray background area of
the Button Bar (it will turn into a hand), as shown:

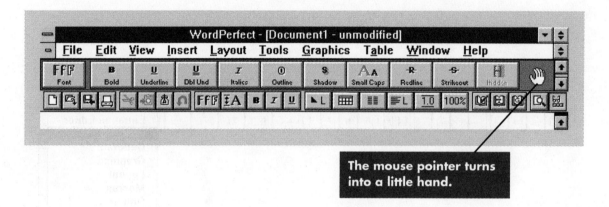

The mouse pointer turns
into a little hand.

2. Click the *left* mouse button and hold it down.

3. Drag the pointer over to the right side of the window (a
ghost image of a rectangle will appear along the right side),
as shown:

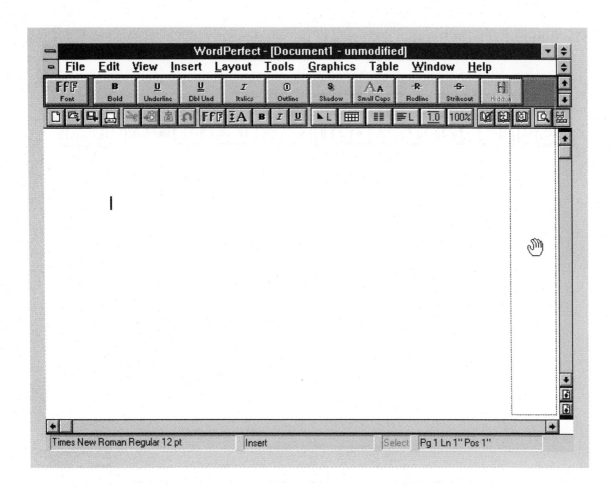

• Note You may notice if you drag the hand pointer near the middle of the screen that the ghost rectangle will turn into a more compact shape. If you release the mouse button when the rectangle looks like that, the Button Bar will appear as a roughly square palette in the middle of the screen, like a moveable dialog box.

Quick Easy

The Button Bar locks into the right side of the window:

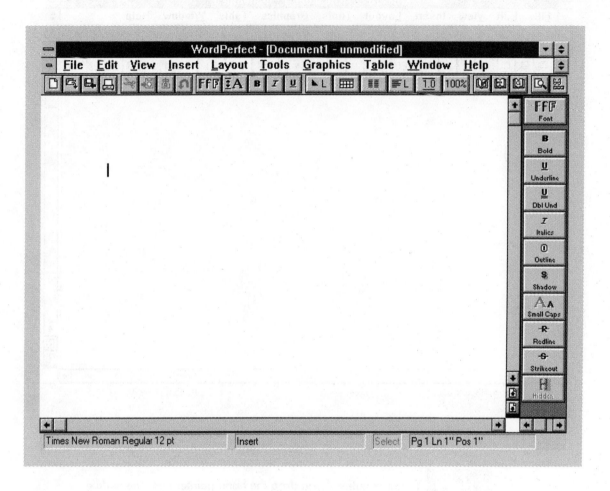

• Note You can also just as easily drag the Button Bar to the bottom of
the screen, or to the left side.

Check out the rest of the Button Bars if you're interested.

Too Many Bars Spoil the Screen

If you'd just as soon keep the screen as uncluttered as possible, then just hide the Button Bar in the same way you displayed it in the first place.

1. Click the View Button Bar button on the Power Bar.

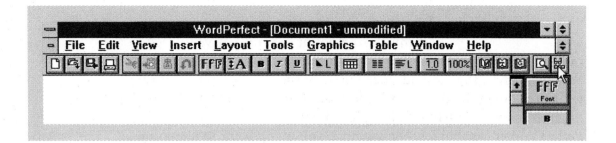

Well, you're done! You can now write, format, and edit documents in WordPerfect. Congratulations.

Where Do I Go from Here?

In this short amount of time, you've learned most of the things you'll ever need to know about WordPerfect for Windows. Even the most advanced users of the program spend most of their time doing the things you've learned from this book. Still, you might reach a point where you want to know a little more about WordPerfect's other capabilities. For example, you might want to learn how to save your place with a bookmark; or how to use some of WordPerfect's advanced printing features, such as printing envelopes; or how to make lists automatically; or how to set up tables and columns to organize information; or how to draw simple shapes or produce charts and graphs; or how to use Grammatik, WordPerfect's built-in grammar checker, in addition to the Speller; or how to find better words in the Thesaurus.

If you'd like to stick with a beginner's approach, learning in short, easy lessons, and trying things out step-by-step, then **ABC's of WordPerfect for Windows 6.0**, Alan R. Neibauer, SYBEX, 1994, is the right book for you. It covers the material in this book with a little more explanation, then continues to explain some of the more useful advanced features.

If you think you're ready for a how-to book that doubles as a reference and covers WordPerfect in depth, try the best-selling **Mastering WordPerfect for Windows 6.0**, Alan Simpson, SYBEX, 1994. It's full of great examples and hands-on steps, and explains everything from the most basic topics to the most advanced.

If you'd like a quick reference book to answer occasional questions, then you want **WordPerfect for Windows 6.0 Instant Reference**, Alan Simpson, SYBEX, 1994.

right justification, 80–81
Ruler Bar command, 97, 99
Ruler Bar for margins,
96–99

S

sans serif fonts, 74
Save As command, 20, 22
Save As dialog box, 17–18,
31
Save command, 16, 19
saving documents
automatic, 22
after changes, 19–20
copies of, 20–22
exiting with, 29–32
exiting without, 127–128
first time, 16–19
before replacing text, 148
screens
blank, 2
WordPerfect, 6
scroll arrows, 60
scroll bars, 40, 52–54,
58–61
scroll boxes, 40, 52–54,
59–61

scrolling
in document lists, 39–40
navigating by, 58–61
Select All command, 65
selecting
for deletion, 120–122
text, 48, 62–66
sentences, selecting, 63
serif fonts, 74
size of fonts, 74–77
Skip Once spelling option,
156
spacing of lines, 89–91
Speller, 152–158
Speller button, 154
Speller dialog box, 154
Start spelling option, 155
starting WordPerfect, 2–7
status bar, 6
suggestions by Speller, 155
Suppress dialog box, 114–
115
suppressing title page items,
114–115
switching between docu-
ments, 44
System Errors, 21

T

text
   aligning, 78–84
   copying, 47–50, 133–134, 139–144
   deleting, 120–122
   editing, 118–123
   emphasizing, 67–71
   finding, 145–148
   moving, 129–133, 135–139
   replacing, 148–151
   selecting, 62–66
   size of, 74–77
   typeface for, 72–74
timed document backups, 22
Times New Roman font, 74
title bars, 17, 19
title pages
   forcing pages for, 110–114
   suppressing items on, 114–115
top of page, moving to, 118
top of screen, moving to, 53

triple-clicking for selecting sentences, 63
Two Page command
   for page numbers, 103–104
   for title pages, 113
typeface for fonts, 72–74
Typeover Mode, 118–120
typing, 8–11
typos, correcting, 152–158

U

Underline button, 67–68
underlined text, 67–69
Undo button, 126
Undo command, 126–127
undoing mistakes, 124–128

V

vertical scroll bars, 58–61
View Button Bar button, 6–7, 160, 165
View menu
   for Ruler Bar, 97, 99
   for two-page spread, 103–104, 113

W

Window menu, 4–5
   for copying between
     documents, 143
   for switching between
     documents, 44
Windows, starting, 3
Windows Applications op-
     tion, 4–5
word wrap, 9–10
words
     deleting, 15, 122–123

     duplicate, 155–156
     finding, 145–148
     moving insertion point
      by, 56–57
     replacing, 148–151
     selecting, 63
     spell checking, 152–158
.wpd extension, 19
wpdocs directory, 38, 41
WPWin 6.0 icon, 5–6
WPWin 6.0 option, 4–5
wrapping words, 9–10